CODING INTERVIEW

Advanced Methods to Learn and
Excel in Coding Interview

ERIC SCHMIDT

Table of Contents

Introduction

Well, now that you have graduated or are done with your diploma/courses – you're seeking to land a job at one of the tech companies. You're dreaming of building your career and climbing the corporate ladder all the way up from beginner to CEO. However, you need to begin somewhere. All the corporate environment and interactions are scaring you and making you nervous.

You want to be prepared and ensure you're loaded with the answers the interviewer will throw your way. Although it may seem like a usual interview for an ordinary job as a desk person – it's not.

You will be analyzed with every skill and competency that makes you a great fit for the firm. Nonetheless, the interview shouldn't be as scary as you might think it is. No bigfoot man will sit across you with a sledgehammer and chop off a finger every time you respond with an incorrect answer.

You may find yourself constantly ruminating on the following list of questions, which is by no means exhaustive.

"Am I expected to walk over my code verbally?"

"How frequently am I expected to speak with the interviewer?"

Oh my gosh, I completely forgot to initialize my variable! Is my fate sealed?

"I'm curious to know what the interviewer thought of my response."

"Would it be all right if I did this?"

And the questions continue to pile up...

You've been daydreaming about this moment since you were a little child, and now you finally have the chance to interview for the job of your dreams. And it all boils down to making a good impression on someone you've never met in the allotted amount of time. The fight is very genuine.

Chill out! The interview will be a breeze for you if the degree you hold or the diploma/course you hold is justified. Having the confidence to go through the interview will be a bonus for you and act as a strong point in your hiring process.

It's a difficult experience to write (functioning) code during an interview, especially when someone is watching your every keyboard to ensure you're doing things correctly. The situation is made much worse by the fact that, as the interviewee, you are urged to verbalize your thought process to the person conducting the interview.

Individuals used to believe that it was physically challenging to think, program, and present all at once, but it has since become that most individuals are just not excellent at coding interviews at the outset of their careers. Studying, putting up a solid plan, and putting in enough practice time will help you become a great interviewer.

Regrettably, the candidates do not get a say in the matter; the firms decide on the ground rules. There is a significant focus on fundamental ideas from general computer science, such as algorithms, design patterns, and data structures; these are the kinds of abilities that a capable software engineer ought to have. You need to enhance your coding interview abilities if you want to get the job, and you need to play by the rules that the game masters have put up.

The bulk of this book is divided into the two parts listed below. You are free to jump to the part of the discussion that most interests you.

- The structure of coding interviews and advice on how to be ready for them.

- Advice on studying the subject of algorithms and suggested exercises for strengthening your understanding of the fundamentals.

Sitting with someone and watching them code can teach you all of this in a short period. Hands-on experience at the keyboard must be at the very least a part of the interview process for any prospective software developer.

The Dissection of a Coding Interview

You might be wondering, "Fine, but what does an actual coding interview feel like?" Assuming that there is a slot of 45 minutes available for the interview, the format will typically be something like this:

- The introductions will take 5 minutes.

- 35 minutes spent coding within a genuine integrated development environment.

- The last 5 minutes are for the wrap-up

Therefore, it is clear that the bulk of this interview should be spent observing the applicant while they solve coding tasks or write code. Remember that the technical interview is only a small part of the whole interview process.

Coding interviews, when conducted correctly, are a useful tool for measuring the candidate's coding ability in a very genuine and quantifiable way. While it is true that other qualifications are also necessary for software engineers, the ability to code well should be a high priority.

Now — let's dive into the book and crack the coding interview for you!

Chapter 1

The Interview Base

Interviewees being considered for a technical position are frequently put through a grueling ordeal that puts their capacity for critical thinking and problem solving to the test. While technical issues aren't included in every technical interview, they may provide valuable insight into how a candidate's strengths relate to the needs of the position they're applying for.

This chapter defines a technical interview, explains why recruiters use them, and provides practice questions and answers to help you be ready for your next technical interview.

Introduction to Technical Interview

Companies employing professionals in fields such as computer science, engineering, information technology, or any other technical field generally conduct technical interviews. Interviewers can evaluate applicants' technical abilities, problem-solving abilities, and critical thinking abilities through the use of technical interviews.

It is standard practice for interviewers to examine a candidate's problem-solving and creative thinking skills during a technical interview by posing a series of logic puzzles, numerical reasoning tasks, or technical evaluation challenges. Technical interviews with prospective employees may be conducted over the phone or via online video conferencing software in addition to in-person meetings.

The Purpose

A technical interview is a test of the interviewee's ability to think analytically, modify existing approaches, and develop novel responses to technological challenges. If a candidate passes a technical interview, it shows they have the skills necessary for the position. During a technical interview, the interviewer may use a collection of technical challenges to evaluate the candidate's problem-solving skills.

Candidates' problem-solving strategies, analytical thinking, and deductive reasoning can be evaluated during an interview. A right response is helpful, but interviewers are more interested in how you arrived at your solution than in whether or not it is correct.

How Does the Hiring Process Work?

In general, the following factors will play into a recruiter's evaluation of your work:

Skills in Analysis

How much guidance did you need to find a solution? Were you able to find the best possible answer? Is there any way you could tell how long it took you to figure this out? How well did you frame the problem and consider the consequences of your choices if you had to develop or architect a new solution?

Coding Proficiency

Can you describe the process through which you took your algorithm and turned it into something a computer can understand? How tidy and well-maintained was it? Was the possibility of making a mistake taken into account? Has your writing style been effective?

Skill with Technology

Can you say you have a solid understanding of computer science and related technologies?

Experience

Have you ever made wise choices when it came to technical matters? Have you constructed any noteworthy or difficult endeavors? Have you demonstrated motivation, initiative, and other key qualities?

Communicativeness

Are you a good fit for the firm and the team? Have you been able to express yourself clearly to the interviewer?

The relative importance of each factor will change depending on the nature of the inquiry, the position being filled, the team, and the organization's culture. For example, the first three may make up the vast majority of a typical algorithm query.

Interview Structures for Technical Positions

The employer has several interviewing methods to choose from when establishing a precise and equitable selection process. Such factors as the position's requirements, the sector, the company's culture, and the info the employer needs from the candidate all play a role in this decision.

Interviewing methods can either be organized or unstructured, depending on how they are carried out. The primary goal of a well-structured interview is to identify key competencies for the open post. Candidates for a certain post are all asked the same set of questions by the interviewer. As a result, the interviewer may more easily evaluate and compare candidates using a consistent standard. Although not all interviewers strictly follow the sequence in which the questions are asked, they must cover all that was intended to be covered.

Most of the time, the information an interviewer needs to make a hiring choice may be gleaned through a well-structured interview. Since all applicants are given identical questions during the application and interview processes, this can be an important defense against discrimination claims during the hiring and selection processes.

An unstructured interview is one in which the interviewer does not predetermine questions or topics to cover and instead enables the candidate to direct the conversation. Applicants may feel more comfortable sharing information in lengthy answers to open-ended questions than they would in succinct responses to closed-ended ones.

Also, an unstructured interview allows for questions to be adapted to a candidate's specific set of knowledge and expertise. Unstructured interviews, on the other hand, might make it hard to compare and rate candidates since they are not given the same collection of questions.

Popular forms of interviews include:

- The preliminary conversation over the phone.

- In-person interviews, which can be either behavioral or competency-based or based on a specific issue, are also common.

- Discussion with a group of experts.

Phone Conversation

A candidate's compatibility with the role and the company can be determined through a phone prescreen interview. Many companies employ telephone interviews as a first step in the hiring process before inviting candidates in for face-to-face meetings. During the preliminary interview, the interviewer should probe the applicant with enough well-thought-out questions to ascertain whether or not they are qualified for the role.

Employers can benefit from doing prescreen interviews over the phone by doing the following:

- Check how well the candidate can express themselves in general.

- Provide explanations for any resume gaps that may have been there.

- Inquire about any lengthy pauses in work or career changes.

- Discuss the candidate's pay expectations openly and honestly.

In-Person Interview

During a conventional interview where the interviewer meets the applicant in person, the conversation may be structured or unstructured, depending on the information the interviewer is hoping to glean from the meeting. One-on-one job interviews often take one of three formats: competency-based, behavioral, or situational.

Both behavioral and competency-based interviews inquire into the interviewee's past actions to better understand their potential. The reasoning is on the assumption that an individual's track record can serve as a reliable indicator of how they are likely to act in the future.

The goal of the behavioral approach, a common method of determining if an applicant is qualified for a position, is to examine their past work history, character traits, and applicable abilities. Using a competency-based approach, applicants are evaluated based on their demonstrated ability to perform essential job functions or competencies.

The purpose of the questions asked in a behavioral or competency-based interview is to ascertain whether or not the candidate displays a certain set of characteristics or abilities. The interviewer does not ask the candidate how they would react in a hypothetical circumstance but rather how they have responded to a similar event in the past. Interview questions based on a candidate's demonstrated skills and experience will likely be detailed, in-depth, and direct.

The following are some instances of behavioral questions:

- Give an example of when you effectively used persuasive language to change someone else's mind.

- Tell me about a time you had to deal with a difficult issue and how you handled it.

- Share an instance when your sound judgment and logical reasoning helped you find a solution to a predicament.

- Share an instance when you had a plan and followed through on it to accomplish something.

- Tell me about a moment when you were required to use your presenting abilities to sway another individual's view.

- Give me an instance in which you were forced to follow a rule or regulation you felt was wrong.

The interviewer might probe further for information if the candidate's responses appear vague.

- Specifically, what actions did you take?

- To what extent did you play a part in this?

- What difficulties did you face?

- Can you please explain your reasoning?

- When you think back, what prompted you to make that choice?

Through the use of a competency-based interview, a potential employer may learn more about a candidate's work ethic and overall professionalism. Here are a few samples of competency-based inquiries:

- How did you get people to open up and share their thoughts and opinions? If everyone chipped in, what was the trick? What did they accomplish?

- Give me an example of how your ability to persuade others via speech helped shape a positive outcome. When you thought about it, how did you feel? What did you take away from this experience?

- Describe a time when you had to convince someone else of your viewpoint despite the fact that they obviously disagreed with you. In what ways did you get ready? Which strategy did you use? I'm curious as to their reaction. What happened?

The situational approach is a method of interviewing that involves providing the applicant with a made-up scenario or events and then focusing on the candidate's previous experiences, actions, expertise, abilities, and talents by challenging the candidate to offer concrete instances of how they would react given the situation stated. Interview questions like this give insight into the candidate's thought process and potential actions.

The following are some examples of questions that can be asked during a situational interview.

- You've recently been promoted to the position of human resources director at a firm with 300 workers, and you're finding it difficult to handle all of the HR administrative tasks on your own. The Chief Financial Officer, your boss, has told you to take a more strategic approach. I need your advice on how to approach this problem.

- Someone you used to work with at your previous employer has applied for a job in your company's accounting department. According to what you've heard, this employee was let go after confessing to stealing from the business, but no criminal charges were filed. You do not work in human resources. In this situation, what action would you take, if any?

- You've applied for a job in cable TV's customer care department. What would you say if a client called to complain that a technician who came to her house to fix something left muddy tracks on her brand-new carpet?

Crowd Interviews

There are two distinct kinds of group interviews: those with the candidates and those with the panel. A candidate who is participating in a group interview will be present in a space with people who would be competing for the same job. Interviewees sit in on presentations about the organization and the role, which may be followed up with questions or small-group activities. Group interviews with candidates are far rarer than those with panels.

Individual interviews with two or more panel members are conducted as part of a larger group interview. Group interviews often consist of a series of questions and answers, although candidates may also be requested to take part in an activity or exam.

There is no one right way to arrange a panel interview; it may be either unstructured or structured. A well-structured panel interview can yield more information about an applicant than a single interview could. Even poorer interviewers may learn from observing. Involving candidates with less experience in the recruiting process through panel interviews might be beneficial.

The ideal number of panelists is four or five since a bigger group could be too frightening to manage. Only one interviewer should take the major role, with the others playing supporting ones. During the course of the interview, all interviewers should be actively engaged, but they must be able to distinguish between their respective duties.

Technical Skills

Recruiters want new employees who can contribute to the company's success from day one. This necessitates locating individuals endowed with the appropriate set of technical abilities.

Several technical abilities call for formal education and practice to achieve mastery. They are generally categorized as "hard skills" as well. In comparison with "soft skills," which are more intangible and difficult to pin down, "hard skills" can always be learned in a class and systematically evaluated to determine whether or not they are indeed useful in the workplace. Technical competence refers to the set of skills and knowledge required to carry out a certain job. They are applicable and usually involve doing anything mechanical, IT-related, mathematical, or scientific. There are many examples, such as familiarity with a computer language, design software, or mechanical machinery and tools.

Possessing job-specific abilities in addition to general technical competence might increase your chances of being recruited or promoted. Technical, hard, and occupation-specific abilities are often transferable between positions, although this is rarely the case.

Job-specific hardware, software, program, application, etc., requirements may naturally differ; therefore, be as clear as possible in your application.

Because some abilities tend to go hand in hand within a certain trade or sector, you may speak of them as a "skill set" or "hybrid skills," depending on the position you're applying for.

Employer's Valued Tech Skills

A study of more than three million job listings led to the compilation of the following list, which features the top 20 most in-demand technical talents. Most employers value coding, data analysis, and social media marketing proficiency.

1. C++

2. SQL

3. Java

4. Python

5. Facebook

6. R

7. Ladder

8. HTML

9. Twitter

10. JavaScript

11. Servers

12. LinkedIn

13. Instagram

14. Network Security

15. Algorithms

16. Big Data

17. SAS

18. SPARK

19. Ruby

20. Artificial Intelligence

A Classification of Technical Skills

Let's delve a little deeper into the classification of these technical skills, shall we?

Big Data Analysis

These days, data is essential for nearly any business to function, whether it is customer information or product sales figures. Even while businesses have easy access to data, they still require workers who can properly gather, organize, and analyze it. Some of the most sought-after data analysis talents by employers are:

- Algorithms

- Big Data

- Analytical Skills

- Calculating

- Data Analytics

- Compiling Statistics

- Database Design

- Data Mining

- Documentation

- Database Management

- Modification

- Modeling

- Quantitative Research

- Quantitative Reports

- Needs Analysis

- Statistical Analysis

Programming and Coding

A candidate's coding experience will be seen favorably even if the position is not specifically for a "coder" or "programming" by most businesses. Learning to code and become fluent in many languages will make you an attractive candidate for numerous positions. Some of the most in-demand technical abilities for IT professionals are:

- Certifications

- Applications

- Computing

- Coding

- Customer Support

- Configuration

- Design

- Debugging

- Hardware

- Development

- Implementation

- HTML

- ICT (Information and Communications Technology)

- Information Technology

- Languages

- Infrastructure

- Network Architecture

- Maintenance

- Networking

- Network Security

- Operating Systems

- New Technologies

- Restoration

- Programming

- Servers

- Software

- Security

- Storage

- Solution Delivery

- Systems Analysis

- Structures

- Technology

- Technical Support

- Tools

- Testing

- Troubleshooting

- Training

- Usability

Some FAQs

"Following my interview, I did not immediately receive a response from the company. Does this mean I've been turned down?"

No, the decision-making process of a corporation may be slowed down for any number of valid reasons. One of the people who interviewed you may not have gotten around to giving you feedback just yet. This is a really straightforward explanation. Extremely few businesses have a practice where they do not get back in touch with unsuccessful applicants.

If it has been three to five business days since your interview and the firm has not responded, tactfully contact your recruiter to inquire about the status of your

application.

"Can I reapply if my initial application was turned down?"

Almost usually, albeit in most cases, you will need to wait a little while (6 months to 1 year). In most cases, a single unsuccessful job interview will not significantly impact your subsequent attempts at landing a job. There are a lot of people that apply to Google and Microsoft and get refused, but then get offers from those companies.

Chapter 2

Behind the Curtains of Big Corps

The interview process at most firms is standard. We'll explain the basics of job interviews, including who conducts them and what they look for in prospective candidates. This data should be used to inform your preparation for and activities during the interview.

A screening interview is often the first step in the interview process. As a rule, this takes place over the phone. The best candidates at selective universities may be invited to in-person interviews.

The Facebook Job Interview

There are four primary phases to Facebook's recruiting process: initial application evaluation, phone interviews, in-person interviews, and review by the hiring committee. While every step of the recruiting process is important, the initial telephone screening (which typically consists of 1-2 rounds) and the final in-person interview are the most challenging and critical (4-5 rounds). The typical interview lasted 45 minutes, and the conversion rate is 16%.

1. You Must Get Beyond the Initial Resume Review

Like most traditional corporations, the initial step in Facebook's employment process entails reviewing applicants' resumes. During this phase, recruiters will examine your application in terms of the position's technical requirements, the institution's educational and experiential needs, and so on.

Although hiring standards vary by position and firm, the basics of crafting a good CV for a position at Facebook are not unlike those for a consulting firm. Three primary guidelines must be followed while writing a resume:

First and foremost, you must demonstrate that you possess the qualities and competencies sought by Facebook.

Employees at Facebook should have the following qualities: leadership potential, critical problem-solving abilities, great written and spoken skills, a "sharp" character, an insatiable curiosity, a humble attitude, and a willingness to take constructive criticism.

Second, make sure your bullet points are clear and focused on achieving a certain outcome.

The best method to brag about your past experiences and present successes is with cold, hard facts. The ideal sound of a bullet is something like:

Thirdly, make sure your language is formal, organized, and direct.

Screeners will get the impression that you are a competent communicator if you use formal, well-organized language that gets to the point. Saving time and making a favorable impression throughout the screening process is facilitated by emphasizing your accomplishments with concrete data and well-organized sections.

2. Get Beyond the Preliminary Phone Interviews

When applying for a job at Facebook, you may expect to go through two sessions of phone screenings: the recruiter prescreen and the technical call screening.

Twenty minutes will be allotted for a recruiter to ask you some questions over the phone. The recruiter will use the answers you provide to these "behavioral" questions to determine whether or not you are a good fit for the position you have applied for.

If you get beyond this first set of questions, the recruiter will pair you up with a Facebook developer for a 45-minute technical conference call. After answering some resume-related questions for 10–15 minutes, you'll have 30 minutes to solve one or two coding problems (on data structures, algorithms, etc.) using a basic online code editor.

3. Succeed in In-Person Interviews

Once you pass the preliminary phone interviews, the next step is the in-person interviews. On-site interviews typically last 45 minutes, and there may be as many as five or six additional candidates being interviewed simultaneously.

There are typically four to five rounds of in-person interviews where two factors—your role-specific fit and your process, collaboration, and cultural fit—are evaluated (firm-specific fit).

When applying for technical opportunities, you should be familiar with both programming on-site interviewing and system layout on-site interview sessions. These are the two primary types of interviews that are conducted for technical positions. At least two interviews will be conducted for each category.

- Whiteboarding solutions to somewhat more challenging data structure and algorithmic difficulties is part of the coding on-site interview process. If you have less experience than others, you should expect to go through a greater number of rounds at the onsite interview for the coding position.

- A System Design Onsite Interview aims to generate high-level design architectures for actual products. The more experienced you are, the greater the likelihood you will participate in many interviews like this.

There is a good chance that you will participate in interviews focusing on collaboration, the process, and cultural fit, regardless of the type of employment you are applying for. The interview to determine whether a candidate is a good match will include various issues, including cooperation and collaboration, dispute resolution, and agile technique or process.

4. Get the Job Offer after Being Approved By the Hiring Committee

Kudos! You've made it beyond the most challenging stage of the interview process: the on-site interviews. Candidate review sessions are now being held, when team leaders and supervisors will discuss with you to decide if you are a suitable match for their teams. If a group is interested in having you, they will notify your recruiter, who will then include that information in your application materials for the hiring panel to review.

A panel of Facebook veterans will then review your application and decide whether or not to offer you a job based on your performance. In most cases, this is only a formality. Each reviewer usually notes recruiting suggestions made during applicant review sessions before the hiring committee session. When there is consensus on a single suggestion, a proposal is made.

The Microsoft Job Interview

Microsoft's interview procedure is meant to be easy and stress-free for prospective employees. Since the organization is looking for people who are truly interested in the position, interview questions tend to center on the candidate's strengths rather than being intentionally demanding. Microsoft's hiring staff has also seen that even the most talented candidates sometimes freeze up under pressure. Microsoft's hiring procedure is accordingly tailored.

So that candidates may be well-prepared and present their best self during interviews, some hiring managers provide practice questions or disclose the questions in advance. What follows is a more in-depth discussion of the interview procedure.

The time it takes to hear back from an employer once an application has been submitted might range anywhere from a few days to many months. Campus interviews might take up to two months, so be prepared to wait longer than you think.

Be patient and optimistic while applying for employment with Microsoft. You should expect a call or email from the employer as soon as they review your application and decide whether or not to schedule an interview with you.

Format of the Interviewing Process

The interview process at Microsoft is not standardized. Teams, groups, and final goods all have a role. However, the standard procedure consists of four or five stages designed to evaluate the candidate's practical, problem-solving, and analytical skills. Interview processes typically consist of the following steps:

Phone Screen

Simply, you would review the applicant's résumé. The recruiter will use open-ended and closed-ended behavioral questions to gauge your leadership potential, adaptability, and interest in learning.

Engineers and Software Developers Needed. The questions on the phone screen are more in-depth and technical, focusing on algorithms and data structures. A code challenge will be presented to you in a collaborative text editor. You'll get 30 minutes to come up with a response, much like a remote whiteboarding activity.

Phone Interview

Phone interviews are conducted in a more official setting and typically take longer than in-person meetings. If everything goes as planned, this will happen within a week or two of your initial phone interview.

Your interviewer will give you an issue to solve and then ask you to explain how you came up with the answer. They may ask for a detailed explanation of your method to evaluate your technical competence and capacity for addressing problems.

Furthermore, they want to know more about your character and how well you would mesh with the group. Effective communication and a professional demeanor are prerequisites for this encounter.

For Positions in the Engineering Profession— Engineer positions can involve a second phone interview with management or a senior developer in the field of engineering. Candidates are expected to have a solid understanding of data structures such as linked lists, hash tables, stacks, queues, and arrays. In addition, there are several other kinds of algorithms, such as mergesort, quicksort, divide and conquer, depth-first search, and breadth-first search.

Interview Conducted On-Site

Now, let's say you've made it to the in-person interview stage; good for you! You have just completed the first required step toward becoming a Microsoft employee. An on-site interview can last anywhere from three to four hours, during which time you'll meet with various team members and participate in one or two interviews.

When interviewing for engineering positions, the first round of testing often consists of a challenge or case study in the field. A written exam measuring your analytical reasoning skills may be administered to you in the form of logical puzzles. To assess your programming skills, you will complete two or three code activities, even if you apply for a non-developer position.

To succeed in a developer role, you need to solve complex problems, maintain attention for extended periods, and write clean, maintainable code. Therefore, most Microsoft developer interview questions revolve around fixing a non-compiling code sample or locating problems in pre-existing software.

The Outline Looks Like This:

Each interview consists of two people: Teams of Microsoft interviewers work together to assess candidates thoroughly and rule out prejudice.

- You'll have one-on-one interviews with the team's managers, leaders, and members, lasting for an hour each.

- Meeting the staff over lunch is often included as part of an on-site interview.

- At the end of each round, interviewers will indicate whether or not the candidate has been hired. If a candidate obtains three "no hires," they may be terminated before their contract is up.

At the end of the on-site interview process, you'll speak with the "As Appropriate," who will decide whether or not to hire you. Usually, this is a senior developer or one of your future peers who will be working with you. You shouldn't ignore this step of the Microsoft employment procedure since they have ultimate hiring authority.

The Human Resource Interview

The final step in getting hired at Microsoft usually involves filling out some paperwork. Within a week of the on-site interview, individuals receive a refusal, acceptance, or an invitation to return for another round of human resources interviews.

During the HR round, you will have the opportunity to meet with a representative from Human Resources (HR). This person may question you on a variety of behavioral and technical topics, such as:

- Why did you leave your former position?

- Which C++ capabilities do you have experience with?

- What differences are there between a linked list and an array in the programming language Java?

As the time nears for your official start date, HR may perform additional checks on your history. This is done to rule out the presence of any underlying abnormalities or warning signs.

The Amazon Job Interview

The first step in getting hired by Amazon is understanding the process and how it unfolds. You should know that Amazon only interviews folks they really want to hire, so you've already made some progress toward a possible position there; the interviews will serve to further evaluate your cultural fit. As for the interview itself, here's what to anticipate:

- Control over Human Resources Recruiters.

- A few phone conversations for an interview.

- An essay of one or two pages is due as homework.

- Six or seven in-person meetings with potential candidates.

HR Recruiter/Phone Interview Coordination

A representative from human resources will often contact you through phone, video chat, or email to schedule an initial interview. Be ready to discuss your experience and why you'd be a good fit at Amazon to increase your chances of landing the job. The initial interview will be conducted through video chat, so they'll need to set it up next.

The recruiting supervisor in charge of your recruitment and other high-ranking members of the appropriate team may call you for a phone interview. You will be questioned to prove that you are qualified for the position. Questioning candidates with:

"Tell me about yourself."

"Why Amazon?"

"Explain the whole lifecycle of a project you've worked on?"

"Tell me about a time when you failed."

"What does a laser focus on the customer mean to you?"

"What makes a client experience great?"

"How do you build trust with your clients?"

"If a client makes an unreasonable request, how do you handle it?"

"To what extent can excellent customer service be fostered?"

The STAR method has been shown effective in addressing behavioral interview questions. When answering any question, no matter how precise, be careful to show how you are using Amazon's Leadership principles.

Test-writing

If you do well in the phone interview, you might well be prompted to prepare for the on-site interviews by writing an essay. It should be one to two pages long and addresses questions such as:

"What is the most innovative project you've worked on?" or "Talk about an experience in which you were able to improve your clients' lives." Keep in mind that no matter the topic or prompt, interviewers will look for evidence of your grasp of leadership concepts.

In-Person Interview

Next, you'll spend a full day at an Amazon office and go through another six or seven interviews. These private discussions will run for around an hour. Members of the team you're looking to join, the hiring manager, and a high-level executive will be among those you meet with.

There are usually only two or three managing rules that each interviewer is asked to focus on with the candidate.

An Amazon "Bar Raiser," as they are called, will be the subject of one of the last interviews. These interviewers aren't members of the group you're trying out for, and they care more about your qualifications than whether you meet any requirements for the group.

They get extensive training to make sure Amazon's employment practices never change for the worse. Those things stand in the way of you getting the job offer, and they're a big one.

Recruitment Conference

When it comes time to decide whether to hire you, everyone you spoke with will do so in a single, central location. Typically, the decision will be made within a week following the last interview. Even though it's too late to change anything at this point, you should still send a thank-you message to everyone you met. Keep your grip on the edge of your seat!

Offer Meeting

After a successful interview, human resources will likely ask about your current and expected compensation. A formal written offer will be made after reviewing your qualifications and the requirements of the position. Human resources may opt to invite the interviewee to an "offer meeting" rather than phoning them to explain the situation. Getting a better deal is not on the table at this meeting.

Verify the References

Applicants seeking upper-level roles at Amazon may expect at least two reference checks and possibly more. An HR manager or recruitment manager often spends approximately 20 minutes on the phone with each candidate. Most employers want to speak with at least two of your previous supervisors or coworkers, or if you had a managerial role, one among your former subordinates.

Amazon Hire Timeline

You probably have many questions about how long it takes to get recruited at Amazon now that you have a better understanding of the application procedure they use.

Since the time it takes to fill a position in Amazon's workforce varies widely from job to job, there is no simple solution to this issue. The lengthier the application procedure, the more senior the post you're seeking. This is because of the extensive management interviews that must be scheduled.

It may take many weeks, or even months, to reach the stage of the recruiting process where you meet with multiple managers to discuss your candidacy for a senior post. This is because the vice presidents and directors in charge of such matters need to coordinate their calendars to meet with you simultaneously.

If you're applying for a high-level position at Amazon, you should expect the hiring process to take from around three weeks to several months. Generally speaking, lower-level roles require fewer hoops to jump through during the hiring process.

The Google Job Interview

Google's interview procedure is between four and nine interviews spread out over around two months. Comparatively, many other firms may do 10 or more interviews throughout the course of a year.

To begin the recruiting process at Google, applicants must submit a video resume and a completed online application. If your qualifications are a good fit for the position you are looking for, you will be called in for a preliminary "screening" call, followed by an on-site interview and, finally, an offer.

To help you prepare for your interview with Google, here are the steps involved:

A Round or Two: The First Phone Interview

A first phone interview may run from 30 minutes to an hour, depending on the position and the availability of the interview team member or manager.

There's a chance the software engineer's phone screen will go on for more than an hour. There is also a coding element, which you will finish while discussing your solutions in a Google Doc. This section is included in the assessment. The recruiter could also ask to see your scholastic transcripts.

UX designers will be tasked with generating an app and high-fidelity mockups in Sketch and developing the necessary information architecture and user processes.

In-Person Interviews

Interviews conducted on-site often last between four and five sessions of 45 minutes each. The interviews range from one-on-one chats to group discussions. Your work history and CV may not be major factors at this point.

Google uses a "scientifically proven" technique called "structured interviewing," which requires compiling a questionnaire list and scoring criteria for each topic. To ensure consistency, the same interview questions are used for all positions being filled.

If you're applying for a technical job, you should be prepared to whiteboard a solution to a problem or write some code on the spot. Candidates using an interview app might choose to do it in their language of choice.

Interview questions for non-technical positions will focus on your experiences and career aspirations through the use of behavioral inquiries.

Proposal

The final interview is often the last step in the hiring process. Your compatibility with the company's ethos and core principles will be evaluated at this stage. Former coworkers and the interviewer will provide you with feedback.

Criteria Evaluation and Final Pick: A selection panel will evaluate your work. Then, after a few weeks, you'll get an offer. An offer letter will be sent to you detailing the compensation, perks, and stock package that will be offered to you. Two weeks are provided to the candidate to accept or decline the offer.

Google's Key Qualities

Google's employment process is more streamlined than those at other organizations, and there are good reasons for that, not the least of which is the urgency businesses must fill such positions to minimize disruption to ongoing work and teams.

In addition, they want to make sure you share their commitment to quality work and positive customer service. What are the ideal characteristics for a Google employee candidate to possess? Here are the top 4:

The Google-Savviness

Generally speaking, Google is looking for kind, honest people who can put the user first, be humble, put aside their ego, work toward goals, and take the initiative. Candidates' abilities to work together, their propensity to take the initiative, and their ability to deal with uncertainty will all be assessed by interviewers.

Competence in Thinking Generally

Google is looking for someone who can think creatively and critically to find novel solutions to challenging challenges. They need people who can handle issues without resorting to a particular method or their prior knowledge, but instead, they use a more "systematic" approach.

Role-Specific Skills

When applying to Google, it's important to show that you know what you're doing and have the abilities necessary to succeed. Therefore, it is essential to understand the nature of your position and determine whether or not you are qualified for it.

Qualities of a Leader

Google wants team leaders that are comfortable with reporting directly to the CEO, owning their work, and collaborating effectively with others. Consequently, these characteristics will be evaluated during your time in the Google hiring process.

When hiring new employees, Google prioritizes these and other attributes. Make sure your values and beliefs align with those of the organization before applying for a position there.

Chapter 3

Getting Ready for the Main Action

To come off as competent and assured, pre-interview preparation is essential. If you take the time to prepare for an interview, you can increase your chances of leaving a good one.

In this section, we'll go over why it's crucial to be well-prepared for interviews, what you may expect, and what you should do to get ready.

Why Is Interview Prep Extremely Important?

Since conducting interviews is a talent, there's no substitute for experience. Learning and researching how to respond to inquiries about your desired position is an important part of interview preparation. You may, for instance, team up with a pal and answer their sequence of questions.

This is a great way to gauge how well you handle unexpected inquiries and how well you respond to queries you haven't seen before. You may also concentrate on your body language, eye contact, and other non-verbal cues when you practice.

Gains from Getting Interview-Ready

Some of the advantages you'll gain from being well-prepared for your interview are as follows:

Adds to Your Ease of Mind

A successful interview begins with thorough pre-interview preparation. Feeling more at ease and less stressed is possible when you are prepared for the questions they may ask. When you feel at ease during an interview, you provide insightful responses to each inquiry.

Confidence-Booster

Your self-assurance will increase as you take steps to reduce anxiety and be ready for the interview. Feeling confident and prepared for the interview is a result of practicing answers to common questions. When you confidently walk into an interview, you'll be more likely to draw from the knowledge and expertise you've gained in past roles.

Get Opinion

Answers to common inquiries can be better articulated after participating in a mock interview procedure. You may learn a lot about yourself and your interview skills from a pretend interviewer. They point out problem areas and provide helpful suggestions for fixing them. A practice interviewer will provide feedback on the following in particular:

- Condensing explanations.

- Explicitly stating what has to be stated.

- A good stance to adopt.

- Upbeat mentality.

Getting Ready for the Interview

The top interviewees always perform the items on this list before each interview to ensure the best possible outcome:

1. Do Your Homework on the Firm

Do your homework about the firm and its background, beliefs, and goals before heading in for the interview. You should go elsewhere if you didn't find the answer on their main page. Review any feedback left by former or current clients, customers, or employees to see if any repeating themes might influence your choice to continue working with them. In addition, it will help you be ready for any questions that may arise during the interview pertaining to the firm.

2. Know the Interviewer

Find out who the decision-makers are at the firm and do some homework on them and the company itself. Find their business-related social media pages and investigate their hobbies. Finding a point of connection with the interviewer might make you both feel more comfortable talking about other topics. If you and the interviewer have a love of hiking, for instance, it will set you apart from the other candidates and make you more memorable to the hiring manager.

3. Write Questions

Most interviewers will allow the candidate to ask questions about the conclusion. Prepared questions at the end of an interview demonstrate that you have thoroughly thought about the position and the firm. Try to think of things like:

> *"How would you describe the atmosphere here at your company?"*

> *"I was wondering whether this position offered opportunities for advancement."*

> *"When evaluating workers, what criteria do you use?"*

> *"Where do you feel that you'll have the greatest trouble in this job?"*

> *"Tell me about the best parts of your job here."*

4. Learn Interviewing Basics

The topics of algorithms and data structures are present in a significant portion of the questions asked throughout the interview process. Whatever the case may be, this is the honest truth. Interviewees often provide us with information on the questions they were asked at other firms, and we've found that algorithm questions account for well over 70% of all questions asked. Most firms will value even a passing familiarity with the following methods and data structures.

- Linked lists

- Hash tables

- Quicksort, merge sort

- Breadth-first search, depth-first search

- 2D arrays

- Binary search

- Binary search trees

- Dynamic arrays

- Big-O analysis

- Dynamic programming

The list's seeming insignificance or overwhelming nature will depend on the reader's prior knowledge and experience. Absolutely, that is the objective. A web developer is more likely to encounter these ideas during an interview than when actually building a website.

Studying these ideas can help you perform better in interviews, whether you are self-taught or have been out of school for a while and are unfamiliar with them. Reviewing this information won't hurt if you already know it.

Surprisingly many interview questions may be answered by asking about breadth-first search or uniqueness counting with a hash table. A knowledge of hash tables and the ability to construct a BFS from scratch are prerequisites.

These skills can be learned, and it's not nearly as difficult as many individuals we've spoken with think. The typically scholarly jargon used to discuss algorithms might be off-putting to some. A modern web app's design is deceptively simple compared to the other items on this list. You can pick this up if you know how to construct a web app.

The book "The Algorithm Design Manual" by Steven Skiena is the reference material that comes highly recommended. These topics are covered effectively and clearly in Chapters 3 to 5. Although it employs C and some mathematical vocabulary, the content is clearly explained. As a bonus, many high-quality algorithm courses are available on Coursera. More specifically, this one emphasizes the ideas that will serve you well throughout the interview.

Interviews are a great place to practice the problem-solving skills you learn in an algorithm course, so it's a good idea to brush up on those skills before going in. Learning about algorithms is a great way to prepare for a job interview.

5. Discuss the Costs and Benefits of Everything

So far, we have discussed the nature of the programming questions that are most likely to be asked in an interview for a programming position. However, you could also be asked questions on system design. These are popular with employers, especially among more seasoned job seekers.

To test a candidate's ability to conceptualize and implement solutions to real-world problems, interviewers may provide questions on system design. Google Maps, social networks, and bank APIs are only a few examples of what may be designed.

The first thing to notice is that you need specialized expertise to find solutions to problems in system design. It's obvious that nobody anticipates you to create Google Maps.

However, they do count on your understanding of the design in question. The good thing is that a majority of these inquiries concern the backend of a website; thus, studying this topic will help you a great deal. Things you should know that aren't on this list include:

- Databases
- HTTP
- Caching
- CDNs
- Distributed worker systems
- Load balancers

If you want to succeed, you must grasp these ideas. However, knowing how these components work together to build functional systems is more vital. Reading about real-world applications of these principles by practicing engineers is the greatest approach to learning more about them.

6. Practice Interviewing

Do a practice interview with a friend or family member who has interviewing experience. Give them a list of inquiries to make about you and your position. Inspire them to come up with their own queries without letting on what they are. Take notes at the conclusion of the interview in case they have suggestions about how you may improve. Repeat the simulated interview once you are ready.

7. Practice

Learning how to respond to interview questions is a skill that can be honed with practice. Since stress impairs performance, this is certainly the case, as interviews are known to be quite nerve-wracking. As with any problem, practice is the key to success. The more interviews you have, the less nerve-wracking they will be.

This just develops as a byproduct of time and practice. It seems that even in just a given job search, many applicants fail their first few interviews before succeeding later on. If you have trouble with pressure, mock job interviews might help you get a head start.

8. Print Resume

Many interviewers still ask to see a hard copy of your resume at the meeting, even if they already have it on file. If they ask, have numerous copies ready before your interview. Further, you can always bring them back to your CV if they have any queries that pertain to it.

9. Ensure Your Outfit Is Cleaned and Pressed

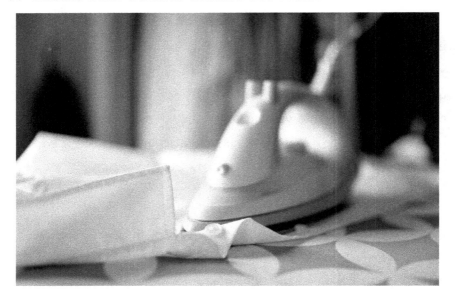

Prepare for your interview by getting a fresh outfit, preferably a day in advance. To remove creases from business attire, an iron and press are necessities. Make sure you have your deodorant and makeup in case you need to freshen up a little before your interview.

10. Note Important Phrases and Names

During an interview, it is not unheard of for a candidate to blank on the name of their interviewer or other important phrases. Put a note on a scrap of paper and slip it inside the folder containing your resume copies. Always feel free to go back to it as you progress through the interview.

11. Silence Your Phone before the Interview

It is recommended that you bring your phone with you to the interview; however, this is not always required. Unless absolutely necessary, you should try to turn it off or at least lower the volume. Make sure your phone doesn't make any noises that might disrupt the interview, such as vibrations.

12. Recall Past Jobs

Common interview questions revolve around getting you to elaborate on relevant experiences from the past. This helps people envision how they would respond if a similar circumstance arose at their company. To prepare for an interview, it might be helpful to recall specific instances from your past jobs in which you demonstrated your strengths. Make use of them as guides in answering specific queries.

Have Faith in Yourself; That's the Real Secret

If you want to create a good impression on your interviewer, boss, coworkers, and anybody you come into contact with throughout your workday, it helps to have a healthy dose of self-assurance.

In this section, let's discuss the value of self-assurance in the workplace and provide concrete tips for fostering it.

Why is it crucial to have confidence in yourself when thinking about your future?

You'll be ready to shine in job interviews and beyond with a healthy dose of confidence. When you walk into an interview feeling good about who you are and what you have to offer, you can relax and concentrate on giving great answers and presenting well-rehearsed presentations. Having faith in one's own abilities helps one shine in professional settings.

Some important advantages of having self-assurance are as follows:

- It helps you think creatively and find answers to problems.
- Colleagues and subordinates can talk to one another better.
- In the workplace, it aids in overcoming difficulties.
- It helps you become a better worker in general.

A Guide to Boosting One's Own Confidence

Developing one's self-assurance calls for introspection and the formation of practices that contribute to an upbeat view of one's own worth. To develop this quality, consider the following:

1. Self-focus

Although there may be other applicants for a position, you should highlight your unique set of skills and experiences to stand out from the crowd.

Create a list of all you've accomplished, learned, and are good at. Understanding the value of your unique viewpoint and experiences requires first accepting who you are as a person.

Determine what you hope to accomplish in your current and future professional capacities. Use them as a guide when you practice for an interview, start a new career, or go about your regular activities.

2. Review Your Past Successes

Make a list of your accomplishments and the targets you're approaching. Write down the actions you need to take and the ones you've already done to achieve your long-term goals. If you take stock of your accomplishments thus far and focus on them, you may find that it gives you confidence.

3. Cultivate a Healthy Perception of Yourself

Adjusting your perspective and avoiding harmful comparisons are good places to start when working to build a more positive self-image. Imagine yourself as you would like to be and work toward that ideal. Imagine successfully doing the duties of the employment you are interviewing for.

4. Face Your Worries

Confront your doubts by thinking about what might prevent you from realizing your full potential. For instance, if you're anxious about whether or not you'll be able to respond adequately to all of the questions the interviewer asks, you could try practicing your responses with a close friend or member of your family. Make an effort to approach folks you don't know in the office and introduce yourself if you feel uncomfortable making small talk.

5. Be Self-reliant

Establish routines of regular exercise, nutritious food, and ample rest. Don't forget to schedule some fun activities — whether they're reviving an old passion or exploring a brand-new one — each day. It's important to take care of yourself, so it's worth thinking about how you may do so even in the office. Some ideas include flexing at your desk and getting regular short breaks.

6. Rejection Should Not Stop You

In spite of the fact that rejection is, unfortunately, a common byproduct of the interview process, learning to see it differently will boost your self-assurance for future attempts. If you aren't successful in landing a particular job, it's important to remember your successes during the interview process.

You could have stood up and answered a challenging question with conviction. In addition to being a rejection, this "no" might provide valuable feedback on your interviewing techniques. It can be worth your while to follow up with the recruiting manager to express gratitude for being considered and getting feedback on your performance.

Remember that rejection in the office is rarely based on anything personal. If you didn't get the job, maybe the person who did had greater experience or talents that were directly applicable to the role.

7. Stay Positive

Reframing one's thought process is essential to developing and sustaining a healthy dose of self-assurance. Reframing how you see yourself might be as simple as thinking about the good things you've done for yourself in the past or how you take care of yourself now. The presence of supportive and encouraging individuals and messages is also crucial to this shift in outlook.

Need of a Top-Notch, Written Resume

The CV is the most important document for prospective employers when making hiring decisions nowadays. It is common practice for employers first to get to know you through written materials before scheduling an interview. How well your CV is written may affect your chances of getting an interview.

You have no chance of winning without a CV, and having a poor one will disqualify you from consideration before you've ever started. That's why a great CV, one that highlights your abilities and sells them to prospective employers, is so important.

What You Bring to the Table Is Summarized in Your Resume

The word "resume" is borrowed from the French for its literal translation: a "summary." It's a perfect description of your resume: Essentially a synopsis of your experience, abilities, and academic and professional accomplishments. It is evidence of your prior accomplishments to present and potential employers. It describes your abilities, education, and job history, as well as the results you have achieved in previous positions.

The letter should also include your career goal (the position for which you are applying) and briefly outline the contributions you can make to the company if you are recruited.

A CV is an advertisement for your skills and experience. The document serves as an advertisement for you, highlighting your individual merits and the value you bring to the table.

Competencies vs. Perks Offered by the Job

To stand out from the crowd, emphasize your value to the company beyond your skill set on your CV. Experts say that, in contrast to resumes of yesteryear, which focused more on the applicant's talents, modern resumes need to demonstrate the applicant's ability to produce tangible outcomes. The employer should be able to easily see the value you provide to his firm after reading your CV. Imagine the company as the end user and yourself as the product. Describe the pitch you'd use to convince a potential employer to hire you.

Employers care less about your amazing skill set and more about the value you can provide to the company. Include these perks in your CV whenever possible. Don't only put "Mastery of PageMaker" on your list of talents if you also have desktop publishing experience. Take advantage of your talents and abilities. Describe your capabilities as they relate to desktop publishing, including your "ability to make appealing brochures at a minimal cost" or anything similar.

Competencies reflect potential, whereas outcomes reflect what you have really accomplished by putting your competencies to use. The company is aware that many of the applicants have PageMaker experience. You should highlight your experience with PageMaker in the workplace and explain to the business what you can perform with this competence. It's qualities like these that employers value most.

Writing Your First Resume/C.V.

Make a template resume with these 7 required sections and use it as a starting point for all of your job applications.

- Provide your name, email, and phone number. You might want to include this information in the header. Individual details include postal and electronic mail addresses and contact numbers. Your age and date of birth are optional.

- If you're not sending a cover letter with your application, you still need to include a personal statement. This statement should be no more than three lines long and highlight your qualifications for the position.

- When listing your educational background, begin with the most recent institution attended and the highest-level credential attained.

- Whether you have a long or short work history, it's important to break each period out into its own section and highlight relevant skills and accomplishments.

- Skills: Potential employers will want to hear about your experience and expertise; keep reading to learn more about what exactly qualifies as a talent.

- Describe your strengths and accomplishments, including any teamwork you've done, any academic or extracurricular projects or events in which you participated, and any hobbies for which you've received recognition, such as a diploma, trophy, or medal.

- Explain what you're passionate about and what volunteer efforts you've made, such as campaigning or sponsorship, to support those causes.

Advice on Creating a Technical Resume

Instead of listing your duties and responsibilities, highlight your most noteworthy achievements in the work history section. This may be seen in the following examples:

- I developed a redesigned user interface that resulted in a 20% rise in customer satisfaction.

- I assisted a group of 15 web designers and developers as a mentor.

- I created and launched a bug tracking and customer commenting system.

- Bugs in customer-facing accounting software were cut by 15 percent after a rewrite.

- I participated in the creation of innovative banking software interfaces as a team.

Suppose you're applying for a managerial position, for instance. In that case, you probably don't need to list your first job working behind a cash register, but you should eliminate any other jobs that are no longer relevant. If you want to provide the potential employer with more pertinent and up-to-date information, you should just mention the most recent ten years of your career history (or your prior three to five positions).

If you have a string of recent jobs but one that isn't directly related to your field of interest, it's preferable to mention that one position rather than leave a gap in your work record.

After establishing a foundational CV, you should modify it to fit the requirements of each position for which you apply. It won't take you long, and it will show the company that you care enough to check them up and read their job posting.

Writing a Resume: What to Do and What Not to Do

Maintain a crystal clear and straightforward format for your resume.

When reviewing a resume, employers spend an average of thirty seconds doing so. You need to immediately make it clear to them why you are the best candidate for the post.

Perform many passes of proofreading on your CV.

Check that there are no problems in the grammar or spelling of the document. Have it reviewed by at least one more person. An employer could have a bad opinion of a candidate based on something as little as a misspelled word on their résumé. It can potentially prohibit you from being hired for the position.

Keep your resume to no more than two pages.

Make sure that the experience you've gained in the most recent years is highlighted in your CV. Any work history or education that is older than 15 years must be eliminated or downplayed. This enables the employer to direct their attention to more pertinent material.

Make sure your resume is tailored specifically to the job you are looking for.

Don't forget to include any relevant job history or notable accomplishments in your cover letter. You can get this information on the employer's website or by reading the job description.

Draw attention to your successes.

Ideally, you'd be able to recall the situations in which you showed your abilities to the greatest use. All of these instances should speak to your accomplishments in the position and the type of worker you are. Typically this would go under the "Work experience" heading on a résumé.

Just tell the truth.

You should never exaggerate your qualifications on a resume. You should not exaggerate your abilities or accomplishments to impress your potential employer. Believe in yourself and your abilities.

Connect your different social media accounts.

Using social networking to advance your career is a brilliant idea. However, if your social media accounts have been used exclusively for non-professional purposes, it's probably advisable not to include links to them on your technical CV.

Try to stick to short, action-oriented phrases. The individual reviewing your résumé may not be the one hiring you. Recruiters and HR personnel may read your resume even if they have no expertise in the topic in question. To persuade, use straightforward words like "directed," "handled," "lead," "established," "expanded," "achieved," "collateralized," and similar verbs.

Verify the details, and be sure to include your contact data.

Your contact information (name, residence, contact, and cellphone) should be included in your resume. Such essential data belongs at the very top of the first page. Verify the accuracy of this data as well. The company will be unable to reach you if this is not the case.

It's important to use a proper email address.

Be sure that your email is legible, brief, polite, and not disrespectful. In most cases, a name-based email address is the most professional option. Don't use any abbreviations, numerals, or other symbols.

Keep the personal details to a minimum.

Do not provide potentially divisive information about yourself, such as your height, age, gender, relationship status, political preferences, or any other personal traits. That way, prejudice won't have a chance to set in. Don't ever, under any circumstances, include your SIN on a résumé.

You shouldn't upload a self-portrait.

Even while photos are the standard in several nations, in Canada they are not. In fact, it can hurt your job prospects and take attention away from your other accomplishments on your CV. You need the potential employer to concentrate on your qualifications rather than your appearance, so, unless asked to, do not upload photos of yourself

Don't get crazy with the gunfire.

If you want your resume to be easily read, use only 5-7 bullet points per section or sub-part. If you format your resume in this way, it will be much simpler for an employer to see your qualifications at a glance. It is important to make good use of bullet points by including only necessary and concise information in each one.

Stop using I and me.

Avoid using "I," "my," and "my." Make your resume sound like it was authored by someone else by writing it in the third person.

Do not merely catalog your duties in this position.

The title you are given in the workplace will describe the tasks you are responsible for. Instead, emphasize your successes by describing how you've applied your unique flair to your responsibilities in the position.

Leave out the details of why you left your prior positions.

Your CV should sell you, your abilities, your experience, and your past accomplishments. There should be nothing negative in there; explaining your departure would do nothing to help your case.

Do not cite any sources.

When a company is genuinely considering employing you, and only you, they will ask for references. Keep references separate and only include them in a submission if asked.

Chapter 4

Primitive and
Non-Primitive Data Types

Primitive is the most basic data type used with the programming language. There are eight different forms of primitive data: Boolean, bytes, characters, integers, long numbers, floating point numbers, and doubles. These different data types provide the basis for all the data manipulation that can be done in a programming language.

The vast majority of computer languages come equipped with support for all fundamental data types. In addition, a great number of languages offer a collection of composite types of data. Language and implementation determine whether or not a one-to-one relationship exists between primitive data types and objects stored in a computer's memory. However, it is generally accepted that the most efficient language structures operate on fundamental data types known as primitives.

For instance, some processors have dedicated instructions for adding integers, and others have the capability of handling multiple characters in a single operation. The C standard makes it clear that "a 'simple' int object has the normal size recommended by the design of the execution environment." This indicates that the length of an int variable on a computer with a 32-bit architecture will almost certainly be 32 bits. Always and only basic primitive types can be value types.

Primitive (built-in, basic) data types cannot be modified by code in most computer languages. The programming language Smalltalk is a notable exception since it permits all types of data to be expanded within a program. This may be accomplished by increasing the number of operations that can be carried out on the data types or even by redefining the already built-in operations.

These kinds of data types have a single function: store the values of a type in their most elemental form. These operations are built into the programming language's type system as the default definition for these data types. These kinds of primitive types are unable to have additional operations specified for them. The Java type system has three more types of primitives, which are as follows:

- The fundamental units of numbers are int, short, long, double, and float. The only thing that can be stored in these fundamental data types is the integer type. Data types like greater than, equal to, etc., are used for more complex comparisons than just simple arithmetic operations like adding, subtracting, etc.

- Bytes and characters are both considered to be textual primitives. These low-level data types can be either Unicode alphabets or integers, and they are used to store characters. Textual data operations include word comparison, string concatenation, etc. However, calculations may also be done using byte and char data types.

- Primitives that may take true or false values, or nothing at all, are called Boolean or null, respectively.

The actual amount of different forms of basic data that may be utilized depends on the computer language employed. Strings, for example, are not just a composite data type but also a built-in data type in C#. This is in contrast to sophisticated dialects of BASIC and JavaScript, in which they are merged into a primitive data type that is additionally basic and built-in.

The primitive data structures are composed of integers, pointers, characters, and floats in the Java language. In general, there are eight different categories of data. The following are some of them:

- Byte data type

- Boolean data type

- short data type

- char data type

- long data type

- int data type

- double data type

- float data type

Char Data Type

This data type can only hold a single character, and that character needs to be surrounded by single quotes (for example, 'E' or 'e') to be read correctly. Another option for displaying certain characters is to utilize the ASCII values. Let's have a look at a straightforward illustration to better understand how it operates.

```java
public class CharDType{

    public static void main(String[] args) {


        char  alphabet= 'Z';


        char a = 25;

        char b = 34,

        char c = 90;

        System.out.println(alphabet); // prints Z

        System.out.println(a); // Displays 65

        System.out.println(b); // Displays 66

        System.out.println(c); // Displays 67

    }

}
```

Boolean Data Type

In computing, true and false are the only two possible values for a single bit of data, which is what the Boolean data type is. This data type may be used to keep track of whether a condition is true or false, and other Boolean data types can be used to record the outcome of several different conditions. Let's put together a little program and investigate how it operates.

```
class booleanDType{

public static void main(String args[]){

// Setting the values for boolean data type

boolean Java = true;

boolean JavaScript = false;

System.out.println(Java);   // Output = true

System.out.println(JavaScript);  // Output = false

}

}
```

Short Data Type

Unlike bytes, shorts are not as big as integers and can only store numbers between -32768 and 32767. The size of this data type is always set to 2 bytes by default. To better understand the short data type, let's look at a concrete example.

```
public class ShortDType{
```

```
public static void main(String[] args) {

    short n= 4453,

        System.out.println(n); // prints the
value present in n i.e. 4453


    }//end of the main function

}//end of ShortDType class
```

Long Data Type

This is a 64-bit integer that stores values in two's complement format. Values for a long data type may fall anywhere between -263 and 263-1, and its standard size is 64 bits.

```
public class LongDType{

    public static void main(String[] args) {

        // a variable named num of long is
created to store the long value

        long number = 1900000000L;

        // The output of the below
System.out.println will print 1900000000
which is the value stored in num

        System.out.println(num);

        // a variable named number1 of long
is created to store the long value

        long number1 = 8934852L;
```

```
        // The output of the below
System.out.println will print 8934852 which
is the value stored in number1

        System.out.println(num);

    }//end of the main function

}//end of LongDType class
```

Int Data Type

This data type can store whole numbers in the range -2147483648 to 21473647, inclusive. When defining variables containing numerical values, the int data type is almost always the one that should be used.

```
    public class IntDType{

        public static void main(String[] args) {

            int num = 5364402;

            System.out.println(num); // prints
    5364402

        }//end of the main function

    }//end of IntDType class
```

Float Data Type

If you require a number with a decimal point, like 8.88 or 3.14515, then you should use a floating-point type. The range of values accepted by this data type is -3.4e038 to +3.4e038 in arbitrary precision. The value must have a final "f" for it to be valid. To further grasp this data type, let's examine a concrete example.

```
public class FloatDType{

    public static void main(String[] args) {

        // a variable named num of a float
type is created to store the float value

        float number =67;

        System.out.println(number); //
prints the floating number value

    }//end of the main function

}//end of LongDType class
```

Double Data Type

Fractional numbers between 1.7e-308 and 1.7e+308 may be stored in a double. Take note that the "d" at the end of the value is required:

```
public class DoubleDType{

    public static void main(String[] args) {

        // a variable named num of double
type is created to store the double value

        double number = 97.777d;

        // The output of the below
System.out.println will print 97.777 which
is the value stored in num
```

```
        System.out.println(number); //
prints the double number value

    }//end of the main function

}//end of DoubleDType class
```

The Non-Primitive Data Types

In contrast to basic data types, they do not come with a specified set of characteristics. Programmers build these forms of user-defined data for use in their applications. Multiple values may be stored in a single instance of this data type.

Take, for instance, the concept of an array, which holds several values. Similar to numbers and strings, classes may be thought of as basic types that can be used to save and retrieve data such as methods and variables. As a consequence of this, the Java community refers to them as advanced data types.

When a non-primitive data type is specified, it will always refer to a storage position in the main memory in which the data is kept; in other words, it will always refer to the memory address where an object is put. This is why you also refer to a variable that stores data of a non-primitive type as an object reference variable or a referred data type.

The stack is home to object reference variables, whereas the heap is where their pointed-to objects are stored. A pointer to the item stored in the heap is kept on the stack.

The following is a list of various forms of data that are not considered primitive. The following are some of them:

- Object
- Class
- Array
- String

Object and Class

A user-defined data type, also known as a user-created data type, is referred to as a class. It serves as a model for the data, which is made up of member variables and procedures. An object is a class's variable that has access to the class's other aspects, such as its procedures and other objects.

Array

A data type known as an array may hold many instances of homogeneous variables, or variables that are all of the same type, in a sequence. They are kept in a way consistent with indexing, beginning with the number 0. Data types that are not basic may be used for the variables and those that are.

String

A series of characters, such as "Javatpoint," "Hello world," or any other string of text, is referred to as a string.

Chapter 5

Methods of Resolving Problems
in Technical Sense

Many of the leading IT businesses use an interview process based on technical questions. Though the seeming complexity of the questions may put off many hopefuls, there are, in fact, methodical methods to tackle them.

Tips for Anticipating Technical Issues

A lot of people who are applying for jobs merely skim through the questions and answers. The analogy here would be learning calculus by reading a problem and its solution. Getting in some problem-solving time is essential. Learning the answers by heart won't get you very far.

Do the following for every issue in this book (and every other problem you encounter):

- Make an effort to find a solution on your own. There are hints at the end of the book, but try to solve it with as little outside aid as possible. It's OK if there are plenty of challenging questions. It's important to consider how much your solution will save time and space.

- It's best to put the code in writing. Syntax highlighting, code completion, and instant debugging are just a few of the perks of computer-based programming. Paper coding does not. Learn to accept this and the slowness of writing and editing code by practicing on paper.

- Use paper to test your code. This includes testing several scenarios, such as the most common ones, the simplest ones, the ones that can cause an error, and so on. You should practice this in preparation for your interview since you will need to demonstrate this skill.

- Enter the code exactly as it appears on the page. In all likelihood, you will blunder quite a bit. Create a running tally of your gaffes in preparation for the actual interview.

- Additionally, it is recommended that you do as many practice interviews as feasible. If you want to practice for an interview with a buddy, you may take turns acting as the interviewer. Even if your buddy isn't a coding or algorithm specialist, they can be able to help you through an issue in the interview process. Experience what it's like to conduct an interview, and you'll also pick up some valuable insights.

Mantras of Solving Problems

In computer science, the focus is squarely on finding and implementing solutions. The first step for every programmer is to learn how a person approaches a problem, known as the "algorithm," and then figure out how to implement that method in code. The last step is to learn the precise computer "writing" syntax needed to complete the task. Machines often find novel approaches to problems that humans would never think of.

A programmer's primary skill is the ability to find solutions. An effective computer problem-solving strategy involves:

- Learn to depict the data that describes the issue properly.

- Find out what has to be done to change the data from one format to another.

Representation of Data

A computer is, at its core, a very naive device. Only integers, characters, Booleans, and arrays (collections of these) are within its ken for the most part. The rest can only be "approximated" by combining the aforementioned forms of information.

A competent programmer will use variables to "encode" all the relevant "information" about a situation. In addition, there are both beneficial and harmful methods of encoding data. The computer can "compute" new data quickly and simply when given good methods.

Algorithm

The term "algorithm" refers to a methodical procedure for finding a solution to a problem. Let's look at it this way. If your 3-year-old niece has never touched a piano before, you'll have to start from the very beginning if you want her to perform your favorite tracks for you. How to find the piano, where to sit on the bench, how to open the lid, which keys to push, in what sequence, etc.

Good programmers, at their core, can articulate the procedures that must be followed to complete a task. Unfortunately, a computer only understands a small handful of actions to do. A computer can do arithmetic operations, such as adding two integers together. However, computing the mean of two integers is beyond the scope of most personal computers. Generally speaking, this is what you need to do to get an average:

1. Add the two integers and store the result in a variable.

2. Enter the result of dividing this new number by 2 into a variable.

3. Tell the remainder of the program this figure.

Hide Complexity with Abstraction and Encapsulation

Encapsulation is a buzzword many computer scientists like to throw about to demonstrate their eloquence. In other words, this is only a label for regular human behavior. The sophisticated word "Abstraction" is added to the mix.

Putting aside specifics is what is meant by talking about abstraction. A forest, for instance, is not just a collection of trees, animals, waterways, and everything else that makes up an ecosystem but a massively complicated one. In contrast, "a forest" is what a computer scientist and the average person see.

Your lecturer has utilized encapsulation and abstraction when he asks you to "Get me a cup of coffee" instead of listing everything he requires. How many actions are needed to get the coffee may be counted on one hand. Getting out of your seat, strolling down the corridor, hopping in the vehicle, driving to the coffee shop, purchasing the beverage, etc. Furthermore, the concept of a cup of coffee itself is vague.

What kind of coffee cup are you bringing, a mug or a Styrofoam one? What's the deal with caffeine? Could you tell me whether it's brewed from concentrate or fresh? Where does it originate, Africa or the United States?

You would soon be rendered completely ineffective if you were required to recall all of these things, which are just way too overwhelming. In this approach, you can "abstract away" the irrelevant information and focus on the essentials.

Now let's discuss "Complexity Hiding." The principle of complexity concealing holds that the finer points are often superfluous. Even a seemingly simple task, such as painting a square on the screen, might need a large number of low-level computer instructions to accomplish in a computer program.

Again, it would be impossible to design engaging applications if the programmer had to re-write (properly) each of those instructions every time the user wished to change the behavior. To make programming manageable, you "encapsulate" the meaning of "draw a square" and "reuse" it in several contexts.

Encapsulation

Encapsulation is the practice of enclosing all data relevant to a notion inside a collection of variables representing a single "object." No matter the specifics of the data, you can then construct a set of functions to work with this object. After then, instead of focusing on the individual components (data) and operations (functions) required to represent the item in a computer, you may instead focus on the whole picture and address the notion at a "high level."

Use of Brute Force

Using as many methods as possible to solve an issue until one works is called a "brute force approach." The brute-force technique will keep testing solutions until one is identified that works.

One may classify such an algorithm as either:

1. The situation is optimized, which means the optimal answer has been found. It may try every conceivable answer until it finds the best one, or it may stop looking once the best one is identified if its value is known in advance.

2. In the traveling salesman dilemma, one must choose the optimal route for a salesperson. In this context, "optimal path" refers to the route that visits all of the desired cities while incurring the fewest possible expenses.

When a good enough answer is discovered, it stops looking for another one. An example would be finding a traveling salesman route that is just 10% less efficient than the ideal one.

Often Time complexity for brute-force techniques grows exponentially. A wide range of optimization and heuristic strategies are available, including:

The word "heuristic" refers to a "rule of thumb" that may be used to quickly determine whether options need further investigation.

One way to improve performance is to rule out certain options before trying them all.

Benefits of Using a Brute-Force Approach

The following is a list of the benefits that come with using the brute-force algorithm:

- The algorithm not only ensures that the right answer is found but also discovers every conceivable answer.

- The method described here has broad applicability.

- It is most often used for dealing with minor issues.

- It's easy to understand and may be used as a reference benchmark for solving a basic issue.

Brute-Force Algorithms Have Its Drawbacks

The shortcomings of the brute-force approach are as follows:

- This method is inefficient since it must solve every possible state.

- To discover the right answer, the algorithm must solve each state without considering whether or not the solution is even possible.

- When compared to alternative algorithms, the brute-force approach is neither inventive nor productive.

Therefore, the Brute force approach is a strategy that ensures solutions for issues of any domain. However, although it is useful for addressing the smaller problems and gives a solution that may act as a reference when evaluating other design strategies, it is both time-consuming and wasteful to perform.

Managing the Fallout from a Failed Coding Interview Question

During your interview for a coding position, it's possible that you won't know the answers to all the questions or that you'll provide the wrong answers to some questions. Here are some things to do if this occurs:

Understand that a Bad Response Is Not Always an Incorrect Answer

Explaining your reasoning while responding to interview questions is crucial in coding. Explaining your thought process to the interviewer is a great way to demonstrate your ability to think critically and dig further into a topic.

To avoid seeming like you don't know what you're talking about, describe the parts of the issue you know. Time is of the essence in a coding interview, so be sure to emphasize your want to keep going.

For example, consider the following: "I realize this isn't the simplest approach, but I'd want to lay the groundwork for a solution anyway. I can rework it and make it faster if I have the time."

Evidence of your knowledge may demonstrate to potential employers that you can work through problems, are persistent, and are honest about your knowledge gaps. Sharing your thoughts with them can assist them to better grasp your position. Some of them may even include suggestions that may lead you to the right answer.

Continue Ahead

You shouldn't allow one bad question or moment of insecurity during an interview to derail your self-assurance for the remainder of the session. It's OK if you don't have all the answers. Make a note to yourself to revisit the issue at a later time and address the subsequent questions with honesty.

Take Criticism Seriously

Coding interviews are often group efforts. In a development team setting, where individuals are responsible for writing code, it is common practice for them to discuss problems they encounter or concepts they cannot quite grasp. Demonstrating that you can collaborate with others to find a solution is an essential skill to demonstrate to your interviewer. If there is time left over after the interview, they may be able to explain a question more thoroughly or point out where you went wrong.

Make Changes for the Better in the Future

You may still learn something from a coding interview, even if you don't end up getting the job. Take the information you've gathered from this test and use it to better prepare for your next job interview. You may go over the material again to ensure comprehension, practice whiteboarding to increase familiarity, or go over the interview questions again to ensure you get them right. Even if you don't get the job for which you interviewed, the process will help you develop valuable skills that will serve you well in the future.

Interact with One Another

Be sure to discuss the methods and procedures you use to solve problems aloud during interviews. Explaining how you came to that conclusion will help potential employers understand your approach to complex situations. Even a bad answer might be a chance to show off your expertise.

Answering Tough Interview Coding Questions

If you are asked a question during an interview that you find difficult or puzzling, the following are some measures you may take to ensure that you provide the best response possible:

1. Clarify Questions with Your Interviewer

It is important to keep in mind that coding interviews are not meant to be seen as tests but rather as chances for cooperation and discourse. Even if it is still essential to present yourself professionally and strongly demonstrate your knowledge, you shouldn't overlook the possibility of drawing from the expertise of the person interviewing you if you find it necessary.

It is preferable to inquire more about the meaning of a question rather than make an educated guess and risk providing an erroneous response. You may learn more about the interviewer's expectations for an answer and prepare thoughtful, well-informed replies by engaging in a back-and-forth with them via questioning.

2. Start with What You Know and Build from There

If you are working on a question that requires you to complete many steps, it is crucial to get started on it even if you do not fully comprehend the issue. If you read a four-part question but are still confused about the third section, you should return to the first two stages.

After you have begun to work on the issue, the significance of the remaining portions may become clearer in the context of the situation. At the very least, you have shown a knowledge of the previous two principles by the time you get to the portion that confuses you, and you still can't comprehend it. After that, your interviewer may be able to point you in the right direction.

3. Be Efficient with Your Time

During a coding interview, it is essential to take into consideration the time component. Suppose you discover that you are spending an excessive amount of time on a particular issue. In that case, you should inquire about the possibility of returning to the subject at a later time. It may be more crucial to answer as many questions as possible in the allotted time, depending on the format of the exam and the number of questions. Work as rapidly as you can without compromising the quality of your work.

4. Make It Easier

Interview questions are notorious for being too wordy and sometimes difficult to understand. The majority of the challenges you could have when building code for real applications won't come up while you're being interviewed for a job. Instead, a potential employer may prepare questions tailored to the interview that are intended to simultaneously assess many facets of your expertise. This might give the impression that the questions have been somewhat manufactured or are unnecessarily difficult, which can sometimes mislead applicants or make it easier for them to misread what the interviewers are asking.

Remember that you should read questions very carefully, and remember that incorrect language might make tasks appear more difficult than they really are. Your anxiousness might sometimes drive you to overcomplicate questions needlessly. Keep a level head when you read, and before you even start to respond to a question, make sure you fully grasp what it is trying to get from you.

5. Defend Your Reasoning

Interviews for coding positions include more than just providing the correct response. They also need you to demonstrate your ability to solve problems and your base level of knowledge. If you're faced with a difficult question during an interview, try talking it out with the interviewer to help you figure it out and to demonstrate your knowledge. Explain your reasoning to the person conducting the interview, and then go to work to find the most effective solution to the issue. Even if you are just partially right, people may still find it interesting to discover how you approach difficult challenges in your thinking.

How to Prevent Other Coding Interview Blunders

In addition to those mentioned above, here are some more frequent slip-ups that candidates for coding jobs should be on the lookout for:

Lack of Forethought and Planning

In addition to making you look more confident, doing thorough pre-interview preparation can make it much simpler to provide a compelling presentation of your talents and experience to potential employers. Examine data structures and algorithms, and brush up on basic coding fundamentals.

Get familiar with the procedures you want to describe rather than relying on rote memorization of code. It's not likely that you'll be asked to write code from scratch during an interview; therefore, it's often better to have a firm grasp of the underlying principles rather than just memorize answers. To be ready for an interview, do some practice problems.

Studying the organization is also essential in getting ready for the interview. Find out as much as you can about the organization's current initiatives, methods, and ethos. If you want to impress potential employers, use your knowledge about the company to demonstrate your interest and enthusiasm for the position during the interview. Ensure your camera, speaker, and other components are fully charged and operational before beginning a remote interview.

Integrity Breaching

Lies about one's proficiency in a language or familiarity with an idea are also widespread in the interview setting. Rather than pretending to have the knowledge you don't have, it's best just to say you don't. The interviewer would appreciate it if you sought clarification on any subject you don't understand since dishonesty is easily uncovered in coding interviews.

Not Double-Checking Your Work

Check for any remaining flaws in your solution once you've finished working on an issue. While it may seem strange to check for errors during a whiteboard interview, it is essential to demonstrate your whole process.

If you're having trouble with your whiteboard code, try creating a brief example input and going over it line by line. Notate on the whiteboard the revised inputs and any additional variables. By following these steps, you may demonstrate to the interviewer that you have a basic understanding of what happens when a computer processor executes a program.

By spending your time and investing effort into troubleshooting your code, you may demonstrate to interviewers the importance you take in generating excellent work. To finish up, just repeat the procedure with some typical outliers. The interviewer will leave with a favorable opinion of you if you demonstrate your level of comprehension.

Chapter 6

The Data Structures

L et's take a step back and ask, "What is data?" before creating data structures. Here's the simple explanation: Data is information formatted for processing and transfer, such as numerical or factual details maintained in a computer system.

Using a computer's predefined data storage, processing, and retrieval structures improves efficiency and productivity. They provide a method for processing data and making it accessible for further processing.

You may think of algorithms and data as the building blocks of any software, program, or application. All information may be thought of as data, and algorithms can be thought of as the guidelines and instructions that transform data into something usable by computer programs.

In other words, keep in mind these two basic equations:

Related data + Permissible operations on the data = Data Structures

Data structures + Algorithms = Programs

Data Structure Is Important

Applications are becoming increasingly data-intensive and difficult to use as a result of advances in technology. The following is a list of problems that are encountered by the majority of apps today:

Exploring Potential

As a result of the massive quantity of data, the searching speed of data is growing slower as data continues to expand. Let's say there's an app that stores information for 10 million users, and every time the system receives a data request, it needs to sift through all of those records. The application's processing performance suffers directly from the massive volume of data.

Speeds of the Processors

While the processor's performance is impressive, it will inevitably slow down when dealing with data in the billions.

System Crash

Due to the simultaneous nature of the requests sent to the server, a poorly optimized system may cause the server to crash because it cannot process the tens of thousands of requests being sent to it.

This data format was created to address the problems mentioned above. You can decrease the search speed with the assistance of data structure, which will ultimately result in an increase in both the reaction time and the speed of the processor.

Data may be structured in such a way that it is not necessary to search through the full set of data in order to find a specific item.

Alternatively, the data that is most relevant to the question at hand can be placed in a higher priority position so that it can be accessed more quickly than the rest of the data; this is just one of many possible organizational schemes for data. Therefore, the data structure serves as the support system for today's highly efficient and rapidly progressing world.

Learning both data structures and algorithms will allow you to do the following:

Create Efficient Programs

When you have a better understanding of the various data structures, you will be able to write code for more effective applications. You will be able to determine which data structure is most appropriate for certain data types and write your code appropriately.

Improved Time and Memory Use

The most expensive components are going to be your time and memory. You will be able to build code that is fast and takes up a very little amount of memory if you make use of data structures.

The Principal Procedures Used in Data Structure are:

- **Insertion** — The process of including any given piece into a specified data structure.

- **Searching** — Locating any specific piece inside the data structure.

- **Deletion** — The process of removing one or more elements from a data structure.

- **Sorting** — arranging all of a data structure's components either in an ascending or descending order, depending on the context.

- **Updation** — modifying any information or element inside a certain data structure or substituting one element for another that is already present in the structure.

The Connection between Data Types and Database Design.

To respond to the question, "What is a data structure? " it is necessary to understand the three primary forms of data.

Abstract

The characteristics of how abstract data operates are its defining characteristics. Graphs, queues, stacks, and sets are all in this data structure category.

Primitive

Primitive data, or basic data as commonly known, includes character, Boolean, pointer, integer values, and floating and fixed-point numerical values.

Composite

Composite data consists of many basic data types integrated into one and contains things like classes, arrays, strings, records, and structs. Additionally, they might be composed of different forms of composites.

These data make up the fundamental elements of data structures. The programmer communicates what they want to do with the data to the interpreter using the specific data type. Data analysts also have several options to help them categorize data structures. The hardest part is working out which structure works for your needs.

How Can You Categorize Data Structures?

What exactly is a data structure? That is a great question! The vast number of terms used to describe it might lead to mental overload and confusion. As you've seen, data and its storage structures may be broken down into a number of distinct categories. Having access to such a wealth of data raises even more inquiries. A linked list is defined as. Exactly what is meant by the term "linear data structure"? To begin, let's define "data structure."

Let's have a look at the categorizations to see if you can make any sense of data structures. It's possible to categorize data structures into three broad categories, each of which is composed of two features.

Linear and Nonlinear Models

Data in linear structures, such as an array, list, or queue, is organized in a straight line. Instead of forming a sequential order, the data in nonlinear structures like a tree or graph links two or more pieces of information.

Dynamic and Static

Static structures, as the name suggests, have sizes and structures that are set in stone at compile time and never change. Predetermined memory space is held in reserve by the array. Memory sizes in dynamic structures may be altered on the fly to meet the changing demands of the running code. Furthermore, the memory's physical position is fluid.

Homogeneous and Non-homogeneous

Like the collections of elements in an array, homogenous data structures have elements of the same kind. Data in inhomogeneous structures are not needed to all be of the same kind.

Having a Solid Data Structure Is Essential

- Information at many organizational levels is provided.

- Simple methods of data storage and retrieval are outlined.

- Allow for group-based operations like new-item addition and finding the item with the greatest priority.

- Assist in the effective administration of massive data sets.

- Offer quick data sorting and searching.

Why Do You Structure Data?

In its most basic form, a data structure serves two interrelated purposes.

Accuracy

Data structure design aims to ensure that the structure reliably processes all input types within the scope of interest. Therefore, the basic objective of any given data structure is to ensure that it is right, with the nature of the issue being solved serving as the determining factor in how the structure is constructed.

Efficiency

The data structure must be effective as well. It has to quickly process the data without using a lot of memory or other computer resources. When working in a real-time environment, the effectiveness of a data structure is a crucial component that plays a role in determining whether or not a process is successful.

Characteristics of the Data Structure

The following are some of the most significant characteristics of data structures:

Resiliency

In a perfect world, all software would respond correctly to any input and run effectively regardless of the hardware platform it was written for. An essential feature of such reliable software is the ability to handle both correct and incorrect inputs.

Adaptability

To create software like word processors, web browsers, and internet search engines, developers need to create massive software systems that can function or execute accurately and effectively for a long period of time. Furthermore, software can change as a result of shifting market circumstances or new technological developments.

Reusability

The ability to be reused and adapt to new situations go hand in hand. It is well known that software development is a costly endeavor since the programmer needs a lot of resources to create the software.

Most potential uses for the program will need its development in a flexible and reusable fashion. Therefore, creating reusable, cost-effective, and time-saving software is feasible by adopting high-quality data structures.

Leaders in Data Structures-Use Enterprises

- ISRO
- NASA
- Amazon
- Google
- Facebook
- Instagram
- YouTube
- Reddit
- Quora
- Dropbox

- IBM

- Yahoo

- Infosys

- TCS

Data Structures and Their Varieties

The following list provides an overview of some of the most essential data structures you should be familiar with. This is by no means a complete collection, and you should feel free to try out various approaches to developing your own unique data structures. But these skills are the foundation for a successful career in computer science or data analysis.

Arrays

Arrays are basic data structures that store elements consecutively. You cannot modify the size of an array because it has a predetermined size and includes values or variables that have the same data type, known as "elements." Since the size of an array is predetermined, you cannot alter the size of an array. In an array, indexing begins at 0, and each item is given a unique number.

The greatest analogy for understanding an array is a weekly pill box. Elements are arranged in a series of little containers lined up next to one another.

To construct additional, more involved data structures, arrays are often utilized. They are also implemented in algorithms for sorting data. Initial values may be assigned to array items at declaration time by surrounding them in brackets.

```
int Num [6] = 2, 67, 21, 30, 96, 22;
```

Brackets should contain the same number of values as the array's declared elements [].

One may talk about a one-dimensional array, a two-dimensional array, or a multi-dimensional array.

Single-Dimensional Array

There's only one column of data in this table. Ascending order is used for storing this.

A Two-Dimensional Array

Data items are organized in rows and columns. Similar to a matrix, this is another name for it.

Multidimensional Array

In a sense, multidimensional arrays may be thought of as an array of arrays. The number of dimensions or indices that may be used with a multidimensional array is not limited to two - as many indexes as necessary may be included.

Restrictions

- There is a hard limit on how many elements an array may contain.

- Information chunks are stashed away in consecutive memory regions that aren't constantly accessible.

- Problems arise when items are included or removed because of the resulting rearranging of other components.

- But linked lists overcome these constraints.

Applications

- Keeping a record of items that all have the same data type.

- Complementary data storage for primary structures.

- Binary tree elements are stored in a fixed-size data array.

- Matrix archiving.

Stacks

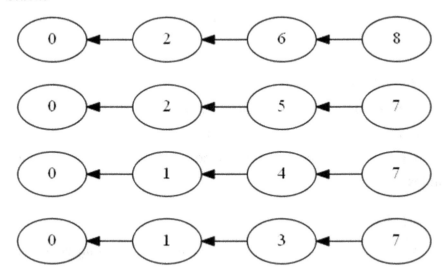

You may think of a stack as precisely what it is: a method of organization. To use a metaphor, it's like fitting building blocks into a tall box.

Last-in, first-out (LIFO) describes how items are ordered in a stack. The item at the end of the sequence will be available first. New elements may be "pushed" to the top of the stack, replacing the currently-positioned one, or "popped" to remove the currently-positioned element.

Stacks are often used in recursive programming to implement function calls and for parsing and analyzing mathematical statements.

Standard Procedures for Stacking Items

The following is a list of typical operations that may be carried out on the stack:

- **push()** is the name given to the operation that occurs when one element is added to another inside a stack. When the stack is completely used up, the overflow condition is triggered.

- **pop()** is the name given to the operation that occurs when you remove one of the elements from the stack. The underflow condition occurs when the stack is empty.

- **isEmpty()** is the function that detects whether or not the stack is empty.

- **isFull():** This function finds out if the stack is at its maximum capacity or not.

- **peek()** gives you the value of the element that is located at the place you provide.

- **count()** gives you back the total number of items that are currently accessible in a stack.

- **change()** is a function that modifies the element that is located at the provided place.

- **display()** will print each of the components that are now present in the stack.

The Applications

- Framework for short-term data storage used in recursive processes.

- Supplemental data structure for inner-operations, function-calls, and delayed/delayed-function execution.

- Handle all calls to functions.

- Different programming language implementations of evaluating arithmetic expressions.

- Expressions with infixes are transformed into those with postfixes.

- In a computer language, checking expression syntax is called syntax checking.

- Paragraph comma splice.

- Inversion of strings.

- All of the issues can be solved by going backward.

- When traversing a graph or tree, a depth-first search is used.

- The OS does its job.

- An editor's undo and redo buttons.

Linked Lists

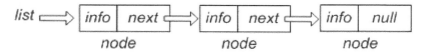

The entries in a linked list are all in some way related to each other and presented in a linear fashion. Consequently, random data access is impossible, and data must be accessed in a certain sequence.

In a linked list, every item is called a "node," and each node has two pieces of information—a "key" and a "pointer"—that identify it. The "next" node is where the pointer takes you next. A "head" at the beginning of the series indicates the starting point of the list. The "tail" refers to the item at the end of the list.

A single linked list may be made, allowing for forward traversal from the beginning to the end of the list. Just as you can make a single-linked list that can only be moved forward, a doubly-linked list can only be moved backward. As a final option, you can make a circular linked list in which the tail's next pointer points to the head and vice versa.

Linked List Classifications

The following are examples of linked lists:

Single-Link Database.

The simplest kind of linked list is called a singly linked list, and it consists of a series of nodes, each of which stores some data and a reference to the next member in the series. The next pointer indicates the location of the next piece of information.

Dual-linked list.

A doubly linked list, or two-way linked list, is the most difficult sort of linked list since each node refers to its next and prior nodes. Hence each node must retain two pointers. This allows travel in both the forward and backward directions.

Recursive linked list.

While a singly linked list's final node links to the first node in the list, a circular linked list's last node refers back to itself. Any node may be used as the starting point for a traversal in a circular linked list, and the process can proceed in either direction.

Doubly Recursive linked list.

Due to the fact that it is a hybrid of a doubly linked list and a circular linked list, it is the most sophisticated kind of linked list. The beginning and end nodes never have null values in a doubly circular linked list.

- The length of a linked list may change on the fly.

- The linked list makes it simple to do actions like inserting and removing items.

- Since random access is not supported, the full list must be combed through to get a single item.

- A larger data size is needed to store references to previous and subsequent nodes.

Upside?

It's less of a hassle to add or remove information.

Drawback?

Performing a search takes a long time and lots of storage space.

The Applications

- Using fixed-size implementations of stacks, queues, binary trees, and graphs.

- Put into action the operating system's dynamic memory management features.

- Methods of doing mathematical calculations using polynomials.

- When a system or program has to execute tasks in a round-robin fashion, a circular linked list is the data structure of choice.

- When the presentation's final slide has been shown, and the viewer wishes to return to the beginning, a circular linked list is employed.

- The forward and back buttons in a browser employ a doubly linked list to navigate between the currently open pages of a website.

- When there are more than two participants in a game, a circular queue is employed to keep everyone in the correct order.

Queues

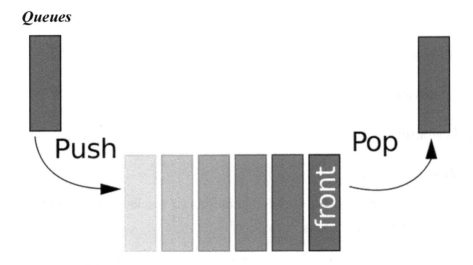

A queue is a data structure with comparable capabilities to a stack, except it follows the FIFO (First In First Out) principle rather than the LIFO (Last In First Out) principle. The concept of a queue may most easily be seen as a line of people standing in a row outside of a building in anticipation of being let inside. The person standing at the front of the line will be the first one to enter the building, and the one standing at the back of the line will be the last one to enter.

In this structure, an item may be enqueued or added to the tail of the queue. Dequeuing an item involves taking it off of the queue's front position.

In multithreading, queues are often employed to manage individual threads, and, not surprisingly, queues are also used in implementing priority queuing systems.

The following are the four distinct queue varieties:

1. Simple Queue or Linear Queue

2. Priority Queue

3. Circular Queue

4. Double Ended Queue (or Deque)

Applications

- To do a breadth search in a graph, this method is used.

- The operating system's job scheduler manages resources like the print buffer and keyboard buffer queues, which are used to temporarily store user inputstore user input and input.

- The scheduling of jobs, central processing unit time, and disk space.

- When it comes to downloading files via a browser, priority queues are employed.

- Communication between the CPU and its peripherals.

- CPU Interrupts that were caused by User Applications.

- In BPO, the consumers take care of the calls.

Trees

Because of how each item is connected to the others, a tree's structure is analogous to a linked list. On the other hand, the nodes that make up a tree are connected to one another in a hierarchical pattern, precisely as you might see in a graphical depiction of someone's family tree. There are many distinct kinds of trees, each of which is better suited to a certain use.

For instance, a binary search tree, often known as a BST, is a kind of data storage that arranges the data it holds in sorted order, with each node in the binary consisting of the following attributes:

- Left (pointer to the left child node)

- Key (the value saved in the node)

- P (pointer to the parent node)

- Right (pointer to the right child node)

There are many kinds of search applications, many of which employ binary search trees. Creating expression solvers and wireless networking both make use of other kinds of trees.

Tree Data Structures Types

The General Tree

No limits are placed on the size of the tree; each parent node may have as many offspring as it wants.

The Binary Tree

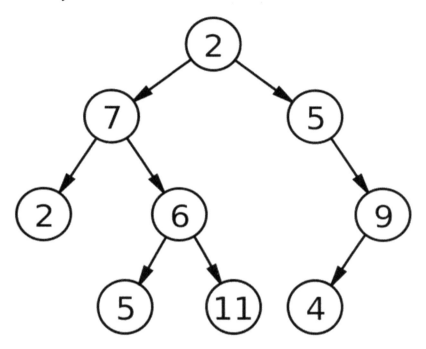

One rule of the binary tree is that no parent node may have more than two children.

The Binary Search Tree

The difference between a binary tree and a binary search tree lies in the additional constraints, such as the left node of the tree needing to be less than the root node and the right node of the tree needing to be bigger than the root node. AVL tree, Red Black tree, and B-Tree Balanced tree are all part of it.

The Balanced Tree

To be considered balanced in a binary search tree, the height difference between the left and right branches must be no more than 1. AVL trees and Red-Black trees are two examples of self-balanced binary search trees.

Upside?

Easily does a search, insert, or delete.

Drawback?

Difficult algorithm for erasing data.

Applications

- Using directory and file systems to implement hierarchical organization.

- Building a site's menu system from the ground up.

- An encoding scheme similar to Huffman's is created.

- Using logic and judgment in video games.

- To schedule OS processes more efficiently, prioritized queues are being built.

- Compilers for computer languages perform the task of parsing expressions and statements.

- As a repository for index keys in a database management system.

- Spanning trees are used when making routing choices in computer and telecommunication networks.

- Hash trees.

- method for finding optimal routes, with potential uses in artificial intelligence, robotics, and gaming.

Hash Tables

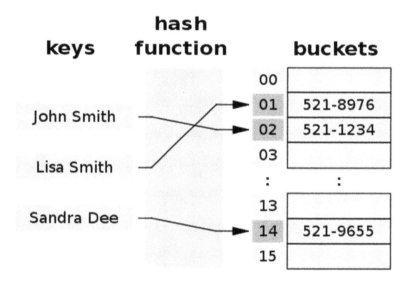

A hash table is a structure that holds information after first associating each value with a key. Using a key to search up values quickly and simply is made possible as a result of this. It doesn't matter how much data there is since this method makes it simple to single out one particular item from among a number of others that are quite similar, making it an effective method for both inserting and searching for data.

For instance, if you attend a certain university, you can be given a one-of-a-kind student ID number. This identification number serves as a key to enable the retrieval of information about you and your student record.

Hash tables employ a "hash function" to translate data sets of arbitrary size to a fixed-sized hash table. Hash values are the names given to the numbers that are returned by a hash function.

It is standard practice to utilize hash tables for constructing database indexes, associative arrays, and when "setting up" something called a "set."

Application

- It is necessary to search things up and input them all the time.

- Applications related to cryptography.

- It is necessary to index the data.

Graphs

Graphs are non-linear abstract data structures consisting of a finite collection of nodes linked together by a directed network of edges. The nodes, also known as "vertices," are the data points in a graph, while the edges are the straight or curved lines between them.

Many types of networks may be represented using graphs, including circuit networks and urban pathways. They are useful for addressing practical issues and may also stand in for virtual systems.

Each Facebook member, for instance, may be represented as a node (or vertex). The information about each user might be stored in a vertex, and edges could represent the connections between users.

Two of the most frequent representations of graphs in data structures are listed below.

The Adjacency Matrix

	A	B	C	D
A	0	0	0	0
B	1	0	1	0
C	1	0	0	1
D	0	0	1	0

The most elementary representation of a graph is an Adjacency Matrix. It is a two-dimensional array of V rows and V columns, and each row and each column represents a vertex. Only "0" or "1" may be found in the matrix. In this case, a value of 0 indicates that there is no route, whereas a value of 1 indicates that there is.

The Adjacency List

It does it by representing the graph in the form of an array (A) of linked lists. The edges are kept as a list, while the vertices are kept as indexes in a one-dimensional array. As a result, it may be concluded that the elements of Ai are lists. Each vertex's neighbors are included.

Structured Graph Operations

Data structure's fundamental graph operations are as follows:

- Vertex Add/Remove - Insert or delete vertices from a graph.
- Insert/Delete Edge Insert/Delete an edge connecting two vertices.
- Verify that a specified value exists in the graph.
- Determine the route that connects the two vertices.

Upside?

True-to-life scenarios are the best models.

Drawback?

Several algorithms are both time-consuming and difficult to understand.

Applications

- Using graphs and diagrams to depict connections and paths in mobile and desktop travel, transit, and communication apps.

- Itineraries plotted on a GPS.

- Connectivity in online communities and other web-based services.

- Software for creating maps.

- Using e-commerce software to showcase shopper preferences.

- City or county governments may learn about their areas' issues by monitoring utility networks.

- A company's resource allocation and accessibility.

- A website's link map is a document that displays the interconnections between pages by use of hypertext links.

- Using neural networks with robotic movements.

Heaps

Just as a binary tree compares the two nodes at the ends, a heap compares the two nodes at the beginning. Over this, the values contained inside the nodes may be organized appropriately. Both trees and binary arrays may be used to represent heaps. However, trees are the more common representation.

There are two distinct kinds of piles. When using a min-heap, the key of the parent is less than or equal to its children's keys. In a max heap, the parent's key is either larger than or equal to the keys of its offspring.

A common use of heaps in algorithm design is creating priority queues and identifying the value in an array that is either the smallest or the biggest.

Application

- Dijkstra's Algorithm is a tool for determining which route in a graph has the fewest number of edges between two nodes.

- The algorithm for sorting heaps.

- Establishing Priority Queues in the System

- One may use a min-heap tree or a max-heap tree to determine which element in an array is the smallest or biggest.

Chapter 7

Algorithms

A n algorithm is a process broken down into a series of steps, each of which describes a list of guidelines that must be carried out in a certain sequence to produce the desired results. In most cases, algorithm development occurs independently of the languages used to generate them; hence, a given algorithm may be interpreted and carried out using any number of different programming languages.

The Pros and Cons of Using Algorithms in Everyday Life

It is not difficult to comprehend. An algorithm is a representation, in a step-by-step format, of a solution to a particular issue.

When a problem is solved using an algorithm, it is first chopped up into manageable chunks or steps; this makes it simpler for a programmer to turn the algorithm into an executable program.

However, the process of writing an algorithm requires a significant amount of time and hence is time-consuming.

It might be challenging to demonstrate Branching and Looping assertions using Algorithms.

Alternative Algorithm Design

The Methodology Known as Top-Down

A top-down method begins with identifying a system's or program's primary components, then decomposing those components into their lower-level counterparts and repeating this process until the desired degree of module complexity is reached. In this, you begin with the topmost module and add modules that are called by it incrementally.

Methodology Known as Bottom-Up

Taking a bottom-up strategy means beginning with the design of the simplest or most fundamental component and working your way up to more complex ones. Beginning at the very bottom, the implementation of operations that give a layer of abstraction takes place.

Sort and Search Algorithms

One of DSA's most important pillars is the practice of sorting and searching for information. Computers are widely used for a variety of tasks nowadays, but one of the most popular is the storage and retrieval of data. The quantity of info and data that can be saved on computers and retrieved using them has, over the course of time, grown into enormous databases.

It is possible to keep and handle information in databases effectively thanks to the myriad of methods and algorithms that have been created. The action of seeking a certain data record inside a database is referred to as searching. The operation of putting the entries in a database into a logical order is referred to as "sorting." Together, sorting and searching make up a significant portion of the research focus in the field of computational techniques. Both of these areas of research are very vital to the study of data structures and algorithm design.

What Exactly Is This Searching?

The action of looking through a group of objects to locate one specific item is known as searching. In most cases, the results of a search will indicate whether or not the item in question is part of the collection. A key field is required, such as a name, ID, or code associated with the object being searched for.

A reference to the sought-after item is provided after the sought-after item's key field has been located. The pointer may indicate the target's location in various ways, including an address, an index within a vector or array, or any other identifier. The user is told whenever there is a failure to locate a matching key field.

The most popular kind of search algorithms are known as:

- Searching in Linear
- Searching in Binary
- Search using Interpolation
- Search using Hash Table

Binary Search Algorithm

The Binary Search Algorithm has a low run-time complexity; therefore, it can complete its tasks quickly. The strategy of "divide and conquer" underlies the operation of this program. In this particular method, you must begin by arranging the collected data in an ascending order. Then you must begin our search for the desired item by analyzing the item that is located in the center of the collection.

If there is a match, the index of the object will be returned. If the center item is larger than the one being sought, the left-most sub-array will be examined. If this is not the case, the sub-array located to the right of the item in the center is searched. This procedure is then used on the sub-array until its size is reduced to zero.

Algorithm

1. Sort the data list such that it is in ascending order.

2. Investigate the center of the fileList.

3. Say FOUND if the destination is the same as fileList[mid].

4. If the target is less than fileList[mid], then the half of the list between fileList[mid] and fileList[last] is thrown away.

5. Get rid of half the files in the list between fileList[first] and fileList[mid] if the goal is more than that point.

6. Keep scanning the trimmed list until the target is located or no more items remain to investigate.

Linear Search Algorithm

The most straightforward search algorithm is known as the linear search algorithm. This search algorithm does a sequential search across all of the objects one at a time to look for the item that is being sought. The procedure continues by checking each item until a match is discovered. If a match is discovered, it is returned; otherwise, the search is continued until the conclusion.

Algorithm

1. Linear Search (Array B, Value y)

2. Initialize iterator I to 1. If iterator I is greater than iterator n, go to iteration 7.

3. Move on to Step 6 if and only if Step 3: B[i] = y

4. Make I equal i+1.

5. Proceed to the next step, which is Step 2.

6. Publish Element y at Index I Step 6, then continue to Step 8.

7. Printed Element Not Found Message

8. Exit

Interpolation Search Algorithm

When compared to Binary Search, the Interpolation Search Algorithm performs far better. It functions based on the probing location of the object that is requested. It functions correctly with sorted data lists with a uniform distribution.

Algorithm

1. Begin your data search in the center of the list.

2. If there is a match, is to return the index of the item and then leave the loop.

3. If there is no match, locate it with a probe.

4. Find the new center of the list after dividing it using the probing formula in the fourth step.

5. Search in higher sub-lists if the data is greater than the middle.

6. Search in the lower sub-list if the data are less extensive than those in the middle.

7. Keep going until you have a perfect match.

The Sorting

The act of arranging the items in a collection into some semblance of a hierarchy is referred to as sorting. A list of words, for instance, might be organized in alphabetical order or according to length. Sorting must be done effectively if other algorithms, which depend on -sorted lists to function, are to be used to their full potential.

The Significance of Sorting

- To display the facts in a way that is easier to read.

- Searching through data should be optimized to a high degree.

The following are the sorting algorithms that are the most common:

1. Insertion Sort

2. Bubble Sort

3. Quick Sort

4. Selection Sort

5. Shell Sort

6. Merge Sort

Insertion Sort

An in-place sorting method based on comparison is called an insertion sort. It is a straightforward technique in which a sorted sublist is kept up to date by adding a single entry at a time. For an element to be put into this sorted sub-list, it first has to identify the area in which it would fit most naturally, and only then can it be moved into place. Therefore, it has its name for that same reason. This approach is not designed to work with very big data sets.

The method has a temporal complexity of $O(n2)$ in both the best and worst possible cases, where n is the total number of objects.

Algorithm

1. Determine whether or not the component in question is the first one.

2. Choose the next element.

3. Compare the item in question with each item on the sorted sublist.

4. Move all the items in the sublist that are sorted higher than the value being sorted.

5. Put the number in

6. Do it repeatedly until the list is in the desired order.

Selection Sort

The method known as selection sort is a comparison sort that takes place in-place. This approach requires us to continually choose the element with the shortest remaining size and then place it at the very end of a growing list that has been sorted. It is one of the more straightforward algorithms for sorting. The selection sort is well-known for being a very straightforward algorithm. In certain contexts, its performance is superior to that of algorithms with greater complexity.

The average andworst-case complexity of this technique are $O(n2)$, where n is the number of elements, making it inappropriate for use with big data sets.

Algorithm

1. Move MIN to position 0.

2. Look for the smallest element in the list.

3. Replace the value at the MIN location.

4. Increase the MIN value to point to the following element.

5. Perform this step as many times as necessary until the list is sorted.

Bubble Sort

The bubble sorting algorithm is the simplest one there is. It relies on comparison, in which each adjacent pair of elements is examined, and if they are not in the correct order, the elements are switched. It does this by iteratively moving over the list of things that need to be sorted, evaluating and exchanging pairs of items at a time, and moving things about if the comparison reveals that the items are in the incorrect order.

The iteration is repeated as many times as necessary until there is no longer any need to exchange elements. This indicates that the list has been sorted. This approach isn't designed to work with really large data sets. Complexity measures for this approach are $O(n2)$, where n is the total number of elements, both in the average and worst case.

Algorithm

```
for I between A-1 and 2,
```

```
swap flag = false

for k=1 to I {

if list[k-1] > list[k]

swap list[k-1] and list[k]
```

Activate the switch flag by setting it to true.

```
}
```

Don't continue if the swap flag is not set. The list has been sorted.

```
}
```

Quick Sort

The method known as quick sort is often used to sort data. This method is sometimes referred to as partition exchange sort and is quite effective. In this particular algorithm for sorting, the array is first split into two subarrays.

One array has items with values that are lower than the pivot value, while the other array has elements with values that are higher than the pivot value. Pivot is a data structure that can compare and split the primary array into two equal halves. An array is first partitioned using quick sort, and then the program recursively calls itself twice to sort the two sub-arrays that are produced by the partitioning. This approach performs quite well when used to very big data sets.

This method has a complexity of O(n2), where n refers to the total number of items being processed. Both the average and the worst-case scenarios have this complexity.

Algorithm

1. Determine which of the indices' greatest values is the pivot

2. Choose two independent variables to indicate the left and right sides of the list (without the pivot).

3. Indicate the low index by pointing to the left.

4. Get the correct points to the high

5. Shift to the right so long as the left-hand value is smaller than the pivot.

6. If the right-hand value is higher than the pivot, then swing to the left.

7. If neither step 5 nor step 6 has produced the desired result, switch the positions of the left and right sides.

8. If the left side is greater than the right side, the place where they intersect is the new pivot.

Quick sort's inner loop is easily implementable on most architectures, making it quicker in practice than other sorting algorithms. It is also feasible to make design decisions in most real-world data that significantly reduce the likelihood that additional time would be needed.

Shell Sort

If you're familiar with insertion sort, think of shell sort as its more generalized cousin. It compares components separated by a few locations to enhance insertion sort. Within the framework of this method, drastic changes are avoided. This technique uses insertion sort on widely separated pieces first then sorts those more closely packed together. The word "interval" is used to describe these spaces. Knuth's formula is used to determine the intervals; it is written as h=h*+1, where h is the interval starting at 1.

The complexity of this method is on the order of O(n), where n is the total number of objects.

Algorithm

1. Set the initial value for h.

2. Separate the list into many smaller sub-lists by dividing it into intervals of equal length.

3. Sort each of these sub-lists using the insertion sorting method

4. Continue in this manner until the whole list has been arranged in chronological order.

Merge Sort

As a comparison-based sorting algorithm, merge sort is able to quickly and accurately sort large datasets. The strategy relies on the age-old tactic of splintering an enemy force to overcome it. Here, the method begins by splitting the array horizontally and then merges the two halves together in sequential order. Although this sorting method is not optimal due to its space cost, it is stable since it maintains the input order of equal items in the sorted output.

Its worst-case temporal complexity of O makes it the most reliable sorting algorithm (n log n).

Algorithm

1. Check to see whether the list has just one item before proceeding.

2. Recursively cut the list in half until no more divisions can be made.

3. Combine the sublists into a single, ranked list.

To do its sorting, Merge sort repeatedly divides the list in half until it can't be further subdivided. Then, merge sort merges the sublists while maintaining the order in the resulting list.

DSA — Graph Based

Breadth-First-Search (BFS) Algorithm.

A graph traversal technique known as a breadth-first search begins its exploration of the graph at the root node and moves outward to each node immediately next to it. After that, it chooses the geographically closest node and proceeds to investigate all of the undiscovered nodes. When doing a graph traversal using BFS, any node in the graph may be regarded as the root node.

There are several approaches to navigating the graph; however, the BFS is the method used most of the time. This approach, used to probe every node in a network or tree, is recursive. In BFS, each graph vertex is classified as either visited or non-visited, depending on which category it falls under. It begins by choosing a single node from inside a graph and then proceeds to visit all of the nodes that are immediately close to the chosen node.

Examples of use for the BFS algorithm:

The following is a list of applications for the breadth-first algorithm (BFS):

- BFS may be used to locate the locations that are next to a particular source location in a larger data set.

- The BFS technique may be used to discover all of the nodes in close proximity to a given one in a P2P network. This method is used by the vast majority of torrent clients, including BitTorrent, uTorrent, and others, to locate "seeds" and "peers" inside the network.

- To generate indexes of online pages, web crawlers might make use of BFS. It's a major algorithm for cataloging the content of the World Wide Web. It begins its journey from the page that served as its source and continues by following the links related to that page. In this instance, each individual web page is treated as a node in the network.

- By using BFS, you can find the minimal spanning tree and the shortest route in a network.

- The BFS algorithm is also used in Cheney's method to replicate the trash collection.

- It may be used in the ford-Fulkerson procedure to determine a given network's highest possible flow rate.

Algorithm

Following is a breakdown of the BFS algorithm's method of graph exploration:

1. Have all of the nodes in G have their STATUS values set to 1 (ready).

2. Set the STATUS of the first node A to 2. (waiting state)

3. Do Steps 4 and 5 until the QUEUE is empty.

4. Remove node N from the queue. Deal with it and make the STATUS = 3 (processed state).

5. Set the STATUS to 2 for all of N's neighbors who are currently ready (with a STATUS of 1). (waiting state)

6. [LOOP CLOSES]

7. Leave

Depth First Search (DFS) Algorithm

The method is recursive, meaning it searches all of the nodes in a tree or graph. The depth-first search, also known as DFS, begins with the beginning node of graph G and continues through deeper nodes until it reaches the target node, which is the node that has no children.

The Distributed File System (DFS) algorithm may be implemented with the help of the stack data structure due to the recursive nature of the structure. The method for the DFS may be implemented in a manner that is analogous to the BFS procedure.

The implementation of the DFS traversal may be broken down into its component parts, as shown in the following step-by-step guide. -

- A stack containing the graph's vertex count should be created first.

- Select a vertex at random, and place it at the top of the stack; this vertex will serve as the beginning point for the traverse.

- Then, you should move a vertex that hasn't been visited yet but is next to the currently most prominent vertex to the top of the stack.

- Steps 3 and 4 have to be repeated until there are no more vertices to visit from the top vertex of the stack.

- If there are no vertices remaining, you need to go back and pop one off the stack.

- Proceed through steps 2, 3, and 4 until there is nothing left in the stack.

The following is an example of one of the applications that can be accomplished through the use of the DFS algorithm: topological sorting may be accomplished by the utilization of the DFS method.

- It is possible to use it to locate the pathways that connect two vertices in a graph.

- In addition to that, it may be used to identify cycles within the graph.

- The DFS method is also used for solving riddles with a single correct answer.

- DFS is used in the process of determining whether or not a graph is bipartite.

Algorithm

1. Have all of the nodes in G have their STATUS values set to 1 (ready).

2. Set the STATUS = 2 flag on the root node A and push it into the stack (waiting state)

3. Repetition of Steps Four and Five Until STACK Is Empty

4. Explore the Nth node from the top. Deal with it and make the STATUS = 3 (processed state)

5. All of N's neighbors whose STATUS is 1 will be pushed into a stack, and their STATUS will be changed to 2. (waiting state)

6. [LOOP CLOSES]

7. Leave

Chapter 8

Interview Questions

Questions pertaining to programming are an essential component of the interview process for the developer role. It does not matter what programming language you are fluent in; it is always required of you to have a solid understanding of the basic ideas behind computer programming.

In every programming interview, the ability to code will always be decisive. In the following paragraphs, you will go through the top 40 coding interview questions you need to be familiar with to ace those interviews and get the job of your dreams.

Now, without further ado, let's get the ball rolling here, shall we?

The following coding interview questions have been broken down into two distinct groups to make your education more manageable.

1. Questions relating to concepts throughout the interview.

2. Interview regarding programming.

Now let's have a look at the first group of questions for the coding interview.

Questions Concerning the Coding of Interviews Regarding Conceptual Understanding

This part of the guide provides examples of questions that may be asked during a coding interview to gauge the candidate's conceptual knowledge.

1. Can you explain the concept of a data structure?

A data structure is a kind of data storage that specifies how information is filed, retrieved, and otherwise handled. Trees, Arrays, and Graphs are examples of well-known and widely used data structures.

2. What is the meaning of an array?

A collection of objects that are kept in memory regions next to one another is sometimes referred to as an array. The items that are kept are all of the same kind. It arranges the data so that a related collection of values may be searched for or sorted easily.

3. Can you explain what a linked list is?

A linked list is a linear data structure, similar to an array, where the components are not necessarily stored contiguously. In its most basic form, it may be seen as a chain made up of a series of nodes, each connected to the one that comes after it.

4. Explain the meaning of the acronym LIFO.

Last In First Out is what the acronym LIFO stands for. It is a technique for gaining access to, storing, and subsequently recovering data. Generally, it retrieves the most recently stored information first.

5. Could you please explain the concept of a stack?

Stacks are linear data structures that use the LIFO approach to perform operations. LIFO stands for Last In First Out, which means the stack must be accessed in a specific order – the last element added is the first one to be removed.

6. Can you explain what "FIFO" means?

FIFO is an abbreviation that stands for "First In, First Out." It is a method for gaining access to, storing, and subsequently retrieving data. When retrieving data, older entries are accessed first.

You have gone through some essential coding interview questions up to this point. Moving further, you will investigate the topic in more depth.

7. Could you please explain the concept of a queue?

In data structures, a queue is a linear arrangement of elements that processes data in a first-in, first-out (FIFO) fashion. In contrast to a stack, the components added the farthest back in time are deleted first from a queue.

8. Could you please explain what binary trees are?

A binary tree is a kind of directed acyclic graph (DAG) in which each node may only have two offspring. A binary tree always contains two nodes, which are referred to as the left node and the right node, respectively.

9. What exactly is meant by the term "recursion"?

A function is said to use recursion when it calls itself in response to a circumstance that causes it to end. This is because it employs the stack data structure and follows the last-in-first-out (LIFO) principle.

A number of the questions coming up in the coding interview are designed to test your familiarity with OOPs.

10. Can you explain the OOPs idea to me?

OOPs is an abbreviation for "Object-Oriented Programming System," which refers to a paradigm that offers ideas like inheritance and classes in addition to objects.

11. OOPs introduce a number of new notions; please describe them.

The ideas presented by OOPs are as follows:

- **Object**. A thing out there that is in a certain condition and acts in a certain way. The term "instance of a class" might be used to describe this phenomenon.

- **Class**. A conceptual structure that specifies the parameters for an object's instantiation.

- **Inheritance**. A term for when an object takes on all the characteristics and actions of its parent. It allows for reusability in the code.

- **Polymorphism**. A mental model that allows for several approaches to completing the same job. To implement polymorphism in Java, you make use of method overloading in conjunction with method overriding.

- **Abstraction**. A theory that solely presents the features of an application rather than its inner workings. To create abstraction in Java, you employ the concepts of the abstract class and the abstract interface.

- **Encapsulation**. A term for the process of enclosing data and instructions inside of one another.

This is a classic interview question for software developers, and depending on the candidate's response, the interviewer may go on to other subjects.

12. Describe in detail what a Binary Search Tree is.

Information is stored in a binary search tree so that it may be accessed quickly and easily. Nodes whose keys are smaller than the node's key value are located in the left subtree. The nodes whose keys are bigger than or equal to the node's key value may be found in the right subtree.

13. Could You Please Explain Doubly Linked Lists?

A subset of linked lists called "doubly linked lists" allows traversal through the data items in both directions. Each node has two links—one leading to the node immediately next to it and another leading to the node immediately before it.

14. Exactly what does a graph entail?

One kind of data structure is a graph, which is a collection of related nodes and edges. In a graph, the ordered pairings, also called edges or arcs, are often used to link the nodes that actually hold the data to the places where that data may be obtained or queried.

15. Can you explain the differences between a linear and non-linear data structure?

A linear data structure is one in which the data items are in straight rows and columns. In contrast, a non-linear data structure allows for connections between every data piece and more than two of its neighbors.

The terms "linked list," "array," "queue," and "stack" all refer to linear data structures. Trees and graphs are two kinds of nonlinear data structures.

16. What is the definition of a Deque?

Simply put, a deque is a queue with two entry points. Element insertion and extraction are possible from both ends of this structure.

17. Could you please explain the difference between an array and a stack?

The stack operates on a LIFO basis, or last-in, first-out. Therefore, there is a predetermined order in which data is accessed, with the most recently stored information being retrieved first.

On the other hand, the elements of an array need not be called in any particular sequence and may be retrieved simply by referencing their index positions.

18. Which algorithm for sorting is considered to be the most effective?

A wide variety of algorithms may be used to sort data, including bubble sort, quick sort, balloon sort, merge sort, radix sort, and many more. There is no such thing as the best or quickest algorithm since each one was created to work well with a particular data set.

19. How does the declaration of variables impact memory?

Depending on the kind of data stored in a variable, different amounts of memory may be allocated for use by the variable. For instance, if a variable is defined to have an "integer type," then 32 bits of memory storage will be set aside for that specific variable.

20. What exactly is meant by the term "dynamic data structures"?

Expanding and contracting in size is a key property of dynamic data structures, which may be used to keep data both organized and flexible. Since it adapts to the scale of the data being edited, it offers a great deal of flexibility.

Job Interview Questions Relating to Programming

The following round of questions is designed to put the applicants' programming knowledge to the test and goes into further depth on various relevant topics.

Here are some common coding interview questions and code samples to help you answer them.

1. Does Java provide a way to flip a string around?

Yes, here's how:

- Create an empty string.

- Measure how long that string is and lop off the excess.

- Iterate through the string's characters.

- Just add them to the new string backward.

  ```
  String str = "kudos";

  String reverse = "";

  int len = str.length();

  for (int i = 0; i < len; i++) {

          reverse = str.charAt(i) + reverse;

  }

  System.out.println(reverse);
  ```

2. How do you tell whether the characters in a string can be read in either direction?

When the order of the characters in a string are reversed without changing the meaning, you call that string a palindrome. It is possible to do this by first reversing the first string and then testing to see whether the resultant reversed string is the same as the initial string.

```java
if (str.equals(reverse)) {

    System.out.println("The string is
Palindrome");

} else {

    System.out.println("The string is not
Palindrome");

}
```

3. How do you count the number of times a certain character appears in a string?

Loop over the string and look for the character in question at each iteration. The count will be updated each time the character is found. This will allow you to determine the total number of occurrences.

```java
int calculate = 0;

char find = 'b';

for (int i = 0; i < length; i++) {

    if (str.charAt(i) == find) {
```

```
        calculate++;

    }

}

System.out.println(calculate);
```

4. What criteria should be used to determine whether or not the two strings that have been provided are anagrams?

If two strings include the same set of letters in a different order, then those strings are considered to be anagrams of each other. Create a boolean variable that, when evaluated at the conclusion of the two strings, indicates whether or not they are anagrams.

First, you need to determine whether or not the length of both strings is the same; if it is not, then it is unlikely that they are anagrams of each other. First, both of the strings should be transformed into character arrays, and then the arrays should be sorted. Verify that the contents of the sorted arrays are the same. If they are the same, anagrams should be printed; otherwise, they should not be.

```
boolean anagrams = false;

if (str.length() != reverse.length()) {

    System.out.println(str + " and " +
reverse + " not anagrams string");

} else {

    char[] anagram0 = str.toCharArray();
```

```
char[] anagram1 = reverse.toCharArray();

Arrays.sort(anagram0);

Arrays.sort(anagram1);

Anagrams = Arrays.equals(anagram0,
anagram1);

}

if (anagrams == true) {

    System.out.println("It is a anagrams
string");

} else {

    System.out.println("It is not a anagrams
string");

}
```

5. **How can you determine how many vowels and consonants are included in a string?**

- Carry out a looping motion through the string.

- If the letter in question is determined to be a vowel, the if condition will cause an increase of one in the value of the vowel variable. In every other case, the consonant variable should be incremented.

- You should print out the values for the vowel count and the consonant count.

```
int numOfVowels = 0;
```

```
int numOfConsonants = 0;

for (int i = 0; i < str.length(); i++) {

    char b = str.charAt(i);

    if (b == 'a' || b == 'e' || b == 'i' ||
b == 'o' || b == 'u')

        numOfVowels++;

    else

        numOfConsonants++;

}

System.out.println("The count of Vowel is: "
+ vowels);

System.out.println("The count of Consonants
is: " + consonants);
```

6. In an integer array, what is the best way to get the items that match?

- Create an array declaration.

- Make use of nested loops to check whether the numbers are equal to or greater than other values in the array.

- If any matched items are identified, print them out.

```
int[] arr = { 1, 2, 3, 4, 5, 4, 3, 7, 8 };

for (int i = 0; i < arr.length; i++) {

    for (int j = i + 1; j < arr.length; j++)
    {
```

```
        if (arr[i] == arr[j])

            System.out.print(arr[i]);

    }

}
```

7. **Describe the process you would use to implement the bubble sort algorithm.**

- Make an array declaration.

- Do an array comparison using nested loops.

- If the array's items are not in ascending order, they will be changed to be in that order.

```
int[] arr = { 1, 2, 6, 7, 9, 5, 11 };

for (int i = 0; i < arr.length; i++) {

    for (int l = 0; l < arr.length - 1 - 1;
l++) {

        if (arr[l] > arr[l + 1]) {

            int b = arr[l];

            arr[l] = arr[l + 1];

            arr[l + 1] = b;

        }

    }

}
```

8. If you were to use the insertion sort algorithm, how would you code it?

Let's suppose that the first item in the array that has to be sorted is already known. The key's second component is kept in a different location. The first two components are now in order. The third piece may then be compared to the two on its left. This procedure will continue until the array is sorted.

```
int[] arr = { 1, 4, 2, 5, 4, 8, 10 };

for (int a = 1; a < arr.length; a++) {

    int c = a;

    while (c > 0 && arr[c - 1] > arr[c]) {

        int z = arr[c];

        arr[c] = arr[c - 1];

        arr[c - 1] = z;

        cc--; }

}
```

9. What are the steps to reversing an array?

Continue looping until you reach the halfway point of the array. It would be helpful if you could change the numbers that relate to the indexes at the beginning and the end.

```
int[] arr = { 2, 3, 4, 6, 7, 8, 11 };

for (int b = 0; b < arr.length / 2; b++) {
```

```
int temp = arr[b];

arr[b] = arr[arr.length - b - 1];

arr[arr.length - b - 1] = temp;
```

}

10. Without introducing a third variable, how would you exchange the values of two numbers?

- Define and fill in the values for two variables.

- Add them together and call the result b.

- The total (b) is then subtracted from a, resulting in a new value for a.

- Finally, swap a and b by subtracting a from a total of b.

```
int x = 20;

int y = 30;

y = y + x;

x = y - x;

y = y- x
```

11. Can you have a recursive Fibonacci sequence printed?

The numbers that follow in this particular integer sequence are known as the Fibonacci numbers:

```
0, 1, 1, 2, 3, 5, 8, 13, 21, 34, 55, 89,
144, ........
```

You have the Fibonacci recursive function formula, so you can apply it to determine these numbers.

```
public static int fibo(int i) {

    if (i <= 1)

        return i;

    return fibo(i - 1) + fibo(i - 2);}

public static void main(String args[]) {

    int i = 10;

    System.out.println(fibo(i));}
```

12. What steps are involved in calculating an integer's factorial?

A function known as a factorial multiplies a given integer by each number that comes before it. Take the number five as an illustration: five multiplied by four times three times two times one equals one hundred and twenty. A recursive function iteratively multiplies the integers up until they reach 1.

```
public static long fact(long i) {

if (i == 1)

    return 1;

else

    return (i * fact(i - 1));

}
```

Chapter 9

The Next Steps You Should Take after Your Interview

What occurs after an interview for a job is just as crucial as what takes place during the interview itself. It is important to follow up after an interview to decrease the likelihood of receiving a rejection letter and increase the likelihood of receiving a job offer. All too often, this stage is either glossed over or altogether skipped. You wouldn't want to waste your time and effort preparing for the interview and then have it go down the drain because you forgot this vital part of the process.

Why Is Post-interview Time Important?

The time immediately after an interview for a job is significant for a few different reasons. To begin, it gives you a chance again to portray yourself in a credible and authoritative light. Following the procedures mentioned in this article, you may not only achieve this during the interview but also strengthen your first impression in the follow-up conversation.

The second benefit is that it allows you to improve your standing as a candidate by ensuring that the interviewer continues to think about you. Third, demonstrating a desire for the job by following up with the appropriate actions after an interview might be a decisive factor in the hiring process if you are competing with other applicants for the position.

Things to Consider and Do Following an Interview

Get a Sense of What Comes Next and How to Get in Touch

After an interview has concluded, it is important to get the hiring manager's contact information and inquire about the following steps. It's possible that doing this will teach you how much time you have to make a choice. The question "What are the following steps?" should not be asked. Questions such as, "How many days do you anticipate you need to make a decision?" and "Would there be a second meeting, and if so, when will you be contacting applicants going forward?" might help you learn more about the hiring process.

Evaluate How Well You Did in the Interview

Note down the questions you remember answering and your answers to use as a benchmark for how well you did. Include the things you didn't say but wish you had since this is an important part of your reflection. You might include some of these items in the follow-up. The objective is to determine the problems and what caused them. It is something to keep in mind for any future interviews.

Send a Message of Gratitude to the Person

A sincere expression of gratitude to the person who interviewed you may have a significant influence. You can either send an email or a handwritten message via mail. It takes longer for a message sent by mail to get to its destination, but the impression it makes is more profound and enduring. You should express gratitude to the interviewer for giving you a chance and for their time. Make it as unique to you as you possibly can.

A personalized letter of gratitude has a far greater effect than one that is written from a template. The purpose of the thank-you letter is twofold: first, to convey your appreciation, and second, to ensure that your name is at the forefront of the employer's mind.

Be sure that the message of gratitude doesn't simply consist of a list of all of the things you are capable of. It should bring to the interviewer's mind the reasons why you are the ideal candidate for the position.

Throw in a few key points you learned throughout the interview to jog the interviewer's memory and emphasize your best attributes. You may talk about a project that you'd be thrilled to work on, how you feel about the culture of the firm, or how your particular skill set would be of the most use to the organization.

Mention a Newsworthy Industrial Event

If you decide to send a letter by email, you have the opportunity to impress the recipient by sending a link to a timely topic that is pertinent to both the interview and the sector in which you are working. You might, for instance, include a reference to a book that expands on your management philosophy if you addressed several management approaches. Suppose you are going in for an interview in a technical field that is always evolving. In that case, you should probably include a link to the online community that you participate in to keep up to date on the latest developments in technical information technology.

Keep in Touch

If you want to be remembered by the person who interviewed you, sending a follow-up note is a good way to ensure that you remain fresh in their memory. Maintain brevity and concision throughout. Sending an email that is very lengthy and full of unnecessary details may give the impression that you are anxious to get the job. It also has a far lower chance of actually being read by the person conducting the interview. They will read it in a shorter amount of time according to how brief it is. Maintaining brevity increases the likelihood that readers will read the whole thing rather than simply skimming over it.

Be sure to follow up with them if the period in which they said they would make their choice has gone. Previously, they may have provided you with a timeline in which they would be making their decision. To ensure that your name is still at the front of the interviewer's inbox after you've left, it's a good idea to follow up with them.

Emphasize that you're eager to hear back from them and that you're ready to answer any more questions or give additional samples of your work if necessary. If you want a rapid response but don't want to ask, "When are you apparently going to make a decision?" then ending with "I look forward to seeing you soon" is a smart compromise.

Summarize the Interview's Most Important Elements on Paper

This action must be taken immediately after the interview while the details are still clear in your head. Take notes on any significant topics discussed or questions addressed and your responses to those questions and topics.

This is of the utmost significance during the first interview since it is possible that you may be asked questions of a similar kind during future interviews. You don't need to repeat the response you gave; instead, you may elaborate on it and inform the interviewer that you've been considering it since the first meeting with them. This is preferable to just repeating the answer.

Furthermore, keep track of everything you intended to say during the interview but were unable to address due to time constraints. You may use this information to your advantage in your next interview or in a thank-you message for your time and consideration if this is your last interview.

Plus, to take down the information discussed, you should examine what took place with an analytical mindset to determine what aspects of the discussion were successful and which were less so. Use this material to practice and improve before your next interview by using what you've learned here.

You will be able to identify any areas in which you need to improve by analyzing your interview. Doing so will ensure you do not forget any key points discussed throughout the interview.

Connect Through Social Media and Professional Networking

After the interview, if you are a member of any social networks geared toward professional networking, try to connect with the person who interviewed you. If they agree to meet with you, it may be because they are curious about what you have to offer. Developing your personal network requires you to do this since it is a vital step. Expanding your network is useful and helps you remain in a position to take advantage of future chances, even if you wind up in a new role with a different firm.

Submit Any Supporting Paperwork

After the interview, you should provide any necessary supporting materials, if any were requested. As part of the preliminary screening process, you may be asked to provide documentation such as a list of references, a handwritten evaluation, or even permission paperwork to do a number of background checks. It should be of the utmost importance to ensure that they are returned in a timely manner.

Get in Touch with Your References

After your initial interview, you should follow up by letting your references know that a possible employer may contact them if you provide references to the potential employer. It is common practice to only provide references for which the individual in question is aware that they are being used as a reference. However, given the current circumstances, if you have any reason to believe that your references may be contacted, you need to inform them so that they are prepared for the call.

Learn to Be Patient and Accept the Situation

Spend the time you have to wait after an interview analyzing your interview evaluation, learning new skills, and immediately preparing for the interviews that are to come after that one. It's always worth reaching out to individuals you know who may know someone at the organization, just in case they have any further information or can introduce you to the hiring manager.

Keep your cool and adhere strictly to the recruiting manager's instructions on whether you should call or email. For instance, if they requested a follow-up email within a week, you should send them an email rather than give them a call, and you should only do so when they specifically ask you to.

Keep Your Cool

It may be quite nerve-wracking to wait for a response from a firm after having an interview with that company. It's important to remember that any given procedure's duration is irrelevant. It is simple to keep running the interview through your head repeatedly, but doing so excessively can lead to aggravation on your part.

You naturally develop a more critical perspective when you go further into an issue. When you factor in the anxiety of waiting to hear back, it's easy to start focusing on how you may have messed up the interview. It is preferable to do an analysis no more than once or twice, send any necessary follow-up communications, and then make an effort to rest in the knowledge that you have done all in your power.

Avoid These Mistakes after Your Interview

The time following a job interview when you're still waiting to hear back may be quite nerve-wracking. After exhausting all of your options, nothing is left to be done. You have no choice but to wait, practice being as patient as you can, and continue taking steps to put yourself on the path to success. Certain dos and don'ts for this situation are similar to those for a job interview. We've compiled a list of five bad moves to make following an interview.

Don't Loop the Interview

In the aftermath of a failed job interview, it's common to dwell on what went wrong and replay the event in your thoughts. The truth is that this is a horrible move. It's not just misleading and depressing to imagine the interview went poorly; it's also not at all how it really happened. Even if your interview went well, you could end up writing the entire thing off if you dwell on the small number of mistakes you made.

Do a once-over on the interview and analyze it, pointing out the positives and the faults. Write down what you did well and what you might improve upon for your next interview. Those are the only two tasks that need to be done, so stop there. There's no use in causing yourself extra anxiety by dwelling on it any longer.

Avoid Making the Recruiting Manager Feel Uncomfortable

Send your note of gratitude to the hiring manager during the first 24 to 48 hours after the interview, but don't contact them again until the day they said they would get in touch with you. There is no need to get in touch with the recruiting manager unless an emergency arises.

The hiring manager may get annoyed if you repeatedly contact them through email or phone to check in on your application's progress or to express your continued interest. It's considerate to wait until the appointed time to contact the hiring manager since they are likely swamped with other applicants' messages. You may get in touch with them again after a few days have passed after that date.

Don't Give Up on Your Job Quest

Nothing is finalized unless a contract is signed. Even if you aced the interview and the HR rep couldn't stop raving about you, it doesn't mean you'll be offered the position. You can never tell whether a better applicant will come up, if someone from inside the company will get the position, or if any number of other circumstances will come into play. Stay at your present employment and keep looking for jobs until you have the contract in hand.

Never Post about the Interview Online

It's easy to fall into the trap of bragging on social media about how well your interview went, posting about how pleased you are for the chance, and then tagging the firm or the person in charge of recruiting. Because you are unaware of the company's social media policy, it is possible that by making posts, you are inadvertently breaking one or more of their criteria. Play it safe by keeping your ideas to yourself, and make your boasts to your loved ones and close friends in private.

Never Ghost a Recruiting Manager

Write an email to the person in charge of recruitment to let them know if you have chosen to take another offer of employment or if you have come to the conclusion that you do not genuinely want this position for any reason. First, you should express your gratitude for their time and the chance, and then you should explain why you've decided to explore another option instead.

They will have a very high level of gratitude toward you for doing this, and they will undoubtedly remember your acts. Because the world of business is much smaller than you may imagine, you will likely see each other again at some time in the future; thus, you shouldn't take the chance of burning any bridges.

Conclusion

Coding interviews are, let's be honest about it, really nerve-wracking experiences. You should enter interviews to make a good impression on our interviewers so that you may get a new position. You are aware that when you go on interviews, you are essentially presenting yourself to be assessed and, in some senses, judged.

Feeling nervous before, during, and after an interview is absolutely natural and okay. Nerves are a perfectly normal and acceptable part of the interviewing process. But how do you get control of your feelings so that you can project an image of someone who is well-prepared, self-assured, and desirable?

A coding interview shouldn't be too much of a challenge for you, seeing as how you've already aced the first round.

If conducting interviews is something you are considering doing, there are certain basic best practices you should follow to enter such interviews with greater confidence. I think it's important for you to first determine your objectives before you start looking for jobs. Think about jobs and firms with room for advancement if you want to become a TPM within the next five years.

If you want a career as a technical architect, you should prioritize working for organizations and jobs that emphasize system design. Pose questions to yourself such as, "What is it that I want to achieve in my professional life?" What is it that I wish to improve upon? What am I particularly enthusiastic about? Finding the answers to these questions will assist you in focusing your job search on the most appropriate employment with the most appropriate firms.

It is essential to keep in mind the importance of applying to a firm for the appropriate reasons. While it's true that many programmers have dreams of working for one of the Big Tech (FAANG+) organizations, it's important to keep in mind that you may have an effect, make a good living, and further your career in a variety of settings. You will have more opportunities for success and fulfillment if you work for a start-up or a smaller company because of the more freedom and flexibility you will enjoy in such settings.

When researching different organizations, you can consult social media websites such as Reddit and Quora and websites like Glassdoor to learn from current and past workers about corporate culture, interview advice, frequent interview questions, and other topics. FYI is yet another well-liked platform on which one may determine their "value" in the IT industry in relation to numerous firms. You may discover more about the role and what it entails by visiting the company's website and connecting with relevant people on LinkedIn.

A candidate who is unfamiliar with the coding interview process should give themselves at least three months to prepare, while a candidate who is already confident in their knowledge of the material should just need four to six weeks.

The time frame might be significantly shorter if you recently interviewed for the position. It's not enough to just put in the effort to prepare for an interview; you need to do it strategically.

Don't bother with specific ideas that you already know well. Be sure to center your preparation on ideas and information that will make you feel strong and ready for the interview. The behavioral interview is an important part of the interview process, and this book provides a road map for how to best prepare for it.

An excellent way to be ready for an interview is to do practice interviews with people you know. To hone your interpersonal and communication abilities, it is helpful to participate in a series of simulated interviews. Mock interviews are a great opportunity to hone your interviewing, question-asking, and conversational skills while also demonstrating your communication, teamwork, and leadership abilities.

Even if you think you know how to tackle the issue, you should be ready for the potential that you don't. If you want to get a job as a programmer, you need to know how to succeed in an interview even if you can't solve the issue.

The process of looking for a job in its entirety might be time-consuming. You may send out dozens of resumes to different companies and never hear back from an employer. If you're lucky enough to get a response and set up an interview, it might take a while before you get an offer of employment.

In addition, there is the time cost of getting ready for an interview. Preparing methodically for a coding interview is crucial. It's recommended that you give yourself at least three months to become ready. It's crucial to allow yourself adequate time for studying, practicing, and comprehending each subject properly, so even though three months seems like a long time, keep in mind that coding interviews are loaded with thick content and difficult issues.

Some considerations will shorten this time limit, including how recently you've interviewed or how well-versed you already are on some crucial issues.

A plan is essential if you want to stay on track and get everything done during preparation. That way, you can go into your coding interview feeling confident and calm, thanks to your extensive work beforehand.

One important thing to remember while preparing for a strategic interview is that you don't have to go into great detail on how you'd really carry out the plan. Everything you'll ever need to know may be expressed as an abstract idea and implemented in your preferred programming language.

Making sure you are learning and practicing the proper subjects ahead of time is also an important part of strategically preparing.

To sum up, keep in mind that the recruiting process at the conclusion of an interview cycle is not instantaneous. The offer may not be extended straight away, but that doesn't mean you won't receive it!

Similar to an engineering project, a well-planned job search entails assembling various parts in a certain order to produce a final product that both you and the client will be satisfied with. Rather, prepare well and then act on that preparation.

Thank you for buying and reading/listening to our book. If you found this book useful/helpful, please take a few minutes and leave a review on Amazon.com or Audible.com (if you bought the audio version).

References

Ankita Singh. (2018, September 26). *Sorting and Searching | Data Structure & Algorithms | Tech Blog*. Tech Blog. https://msatechnosoft.in/blog/searching-sorting-data-structure-algorithms/

Doyle, A. (2013, November 10). *Technical Skills List and Examples*. The Balance Careers; The Balance. https://www.thebalancecareers.com/technical-skills-list-2063775

Indeed Editorial Team. (2021, November 29). *Technical Resume Writing: Tips and Examples*. Indeed Career Guide. https://www.indeed.com/career-advice/resumes-cover-letters/technical-resume-tips

Indeed Editorial Team. (2022, August 8). *15 Things to Do Before an Interview*. Indeed Career Guide. https://www.indeed.com/career-advice/interviewing/what-to-do-before-an-interview

Java T Point. (2011). *BFS Algorithm - javatpoint*. Www.javatpoint.com. https://www.javatpoint.com/breadth-first-search-algorithm

Java T Point. (2015). *DS | Types of Queues - javatpoint.*
Www.javatpoint.com. https://www.javatpoint.com/ds-types-
of-queues

Java T Point. (2017). *DS Stack - javatpoint.* Www.javatpoint.com.
https://www.javatpoint.com/data-structure-stack

Java T Point. (2021, June 23). *Primitive Data Type - javatpoint.*
Www.javatpoint.com.
https://www.javatpoint.com/primitive-data-type

Java T Point. (2022, May 11). *DFS Algorithm - javatpoint.*
Www.javatpoint.com. https://www.javatpoint.com/depth-
first-search-algorithm

Problem Solving. (2012). Www.cs.utah.edu.
https://www.cs.utah.edu/~germain/PPS/Topics/problem_sol
ving.html

SHRM. (2019, April 30). *Interviewing Candidates for Employment.*
SHRM; SHRM.
https://www.shrm.org/resourcesandtools/tools-and-
samples/toolkits/pages/interviewingcandidatesforemployme
nt.aspx

Simplilearn. (2021, May 17). *What Is Data Structure: Types,
Classifications and Applications.* Simplilearn.com.
https://www.simplilearn.com/tutorials/data-structure-
tutorial/what-is-data-structure

?